D1561816

SAN FRANCISCO GIANTS
WHERE HAVE YOU GONE?

SAN FRANCISCO GIANTS
WHERE HAVE YOU GONE?

MATT JOHANSON AND WYLIE WONG

FOREWORD BY JON MILLER

SPORTS
PUBLISHING

Sports Publishing books may be purchased in bulk at special discounts for sales promotion, corporate gifts, fund-raising, or educational purposes. Special editions can also be created to specifications. For details, contact the Special Sales Department, Sports Publishing, 307 West 36th Street, 11th Floor, New York, NY 10018 or sportspubbooks@skyhorsepublishing.com.

Sports Publishing® is a registered trademark of Skyhorse Publishing, Inc.®, a Delaware corporation.

Visit our website at www.sportspubbooks.com.

10 9 8 7 6 5 4 3 2 1

Library of Congress Cataloging-in-Publication Data is available on file.

ISBN: 978-1-61321-359-9

Printed in the United States of America

For my family, friends and Giants fans everywhere. —M.J.

*For my wife, Miiko, whose passion for life inspires me,
and my parents, Frances and Jason, for taking me to my
first Giants game at Candlestick many years ago.* —W.W.

CONTENTS

Editor's note: In addition to adding new material at the end of the book, the authors have worked to bring the chapters throughout the text up to date from the first edition, published in 2005. However, they have also preserved the majority of the original quotes and much of the original text where appropriate.

FOREWORD

Before a Giants home game one evening in the summer of 2000, I walked into Clubhouse Manager Mike Murphy's office adjacent to the entrance of the Giants clubhouse. His office is always a gathering place for baseball luminaries, especially former Giants, many of whom have known "Murph" since 1958, the year the Giants came to San Francisco and the year Murph became a Giants employee.

This particular day, though, was rather special as I walked in to discover Willie Mays, Willie McCovey, and Orlando Cepeda sitting in there. I listened in as these three all-time Giants greats (and all Hall of Famers) told one great story after another. As I listened, I started to mentally tally just how many home runs were represented in that office: 1,560. Besides the Hall of Fame in Cooperstown, how many rooms could you just stroll into and be in the company of that many big league big flies? Just then, who should walk in but Barry Bonds. That brought the current total in the room to more than 2,000 homers.

Although I was already more than aware of the Giants' rich and storied history, I was in awe at having that fact so powerfully demonstrated in such a living, breathing way.

As a Major League Baseball broadcaster I've had the special opportunity of meeting and getting to know these former Giants greats. I've not only been able to hear stories of what all was really happening in those Giants clubhouses of the past, but to also find out what these guys are doing now. With that in mind, I can say that *San Francisco Giants: Where Have You Gone?* is the perfect addition to the baseball library of any Giants fan.

One of the most memorable nights of my childhood came on April 16, 1962. My dad, Gerald Miller, and my Godfather, Keith Allen, took me to my first Major League Baseball game at Candlestick Park. I know how strong an effect that game had on me simply because the memories of that night have remained so vivid for these last 43 years. To wit, I can still tell you not only the extraordinary final score—Giants over the Dodgers, 19-8—but also the final game totals. The Dodgers out-hit the Giants, 15-12, and yet lost by 11 runs! The paid attendance was 32,819. Billy O'Dell pitched a complete game 15-hitter. Felipe Alou hit the first home run I ever saw, and Mays and Jimmy Davenport also went deep.

I am happy to say that the Giants current ownership has a profound sense of the history of the franchise and employs many of these former greats—

including all three of the guys who homered in my first game—which is one of the reasons we see so many of them at the ballpark!

Despite the colorful tradition of Giants baseball, they nearly became the Tampa Bay Giants after the 1992 season. We know well how Peter Magowan and a group of civic-minded investors banded together to keep the Giants here and later built a ballpark that instantly became a San Francisco landmark on the waterfront. But years before, the Giants almost moved to Toronto back in 1976. That's when Bob Lurie bought the team, with Bud Herseth, to save the team for San Francisco (remember, they were buying a team that had drawn only about 500,000 fans in each of the two previous seasons!).

As you reconnect with former Giants within these pages, you'll be able to refresh your memory about just how close they came to leaving then and why Lurie finally, in exasperation, nearly sold the team to Florida in '92.

Now, as you can imagine, I'm constantly being asked "Whatever happened to ol' Mike Krukow and Duane Kuiper?" I'm happy to report *even that* is answered in this book! (And hey, what a shock to read they have a baseball video game out, although I'm sure it's not in the same league with ESPN Major League Baseball 2K5....with Jon Miller and Joe Morgan!).

Yes, like you, I have my special Giants memories. Now, let *San Francisco Giants: Where Have You Gone?* help you relive some of those great days and nights of the past while also bringing to life many of your former Giants favorites in their current lives. Enjoy!

—Jon Miller
Voice of the Giants
and Hall of Famer

ACKNOWLEDGMENTS

This book would not have been possible without the contributions of many people.

The authors wish to thank position players Blake Rhodes, Jim Moorehead, Maria Jacinto, Mario Alioto, Bertha Fajardo, Alison Vidal, Luis Torres and Missy Mikulecky of the Giants, Mike Swanson and Susan Webner of the Arizona Diamondbacks, and Debbie Gallas and Jim Young of the Oakland Athletics for facilitating access, interviews and photography.

Special thanks go to pinch hitter Bob Leung for skillfully interviewing members of the Detroit Tigers, smashing a clutch home run for the Roger Craig chapter.

We're grateful to utility players John Dunphy, Susan Song, Hallie Jaramillo, Haseeb Sadat, Athena Gianopoulos, Ronnie Spencer, Sean Ryan and Linnae Johansson for valuable "off the bench" assistance in research and photography.

Thanks also to bullpen pitchers Mark Gonzales of the *Arizona Republic*, Jim Graham, Sherman Wan and Dan Wong for their support and suggestions.

Managers Karen Johanson and Miiko Mentz provided patient support and encouragement for the duration of the extra-innings project.

Most of all, we thank the many Giants players, their family members, friends and associates, and the team's current and former owners, executives, managers and broadcasters, who granted their time and insights in more than 100 interviews for this book.

DARYL SPENCER

BIG IN JAPAN

Before Godzilla, there was the Monster in Japan. Daryl Spencer, a 1950s Giants infielder who hit the team's first-ever home run in San Francisco, played the last seven years of his career in Japan, where he became famous, not only because of his power hitting, but because of his fun-loving, outgoing personality.

When Spencer wasn't smacking home runs, he was pulling odd, but funny stunts on the field during games, like the time he walked onto the on-deck circle, dressed in T-shirt and shorts, or the time he held a bat upside down in the batter's box to protest the other team's decision to pitch around him. He even introduced aggressive base running to Japanese baseball by taking out a second baseman to prevent a double play and colliding with a catcher on a play at the plate, two plays that changed Japanese baseball forever.

While Yankees outfielder Hideki Matsui was nicknamed "Godzilla" in Japan for swatting monstrous home runs, the Japanese fans and media called Spencer "the Monster," not for his home runs or his physical play, but because he towered over everyone.

"They called me 'the Monster' because I was bigger than the Japanese," recalled Spencer, who stands 6-foot-3. "Back then, I bet not two players in the whole league were 6-foot-tall."

Spencer, who played for the Giants from 1952 to 1959, resurrected his career in Japan after he was released by two teams, the Los Angeles Dodgers and the Cincinnati Reds, in 1963. Spencer thought his baseball career was over, but several teams from Japan recruited him. He signed with the Hankyu Braves in 1964 and became part of the first wave of Americans who crossed the Pacific Ocean to play ball and extend their careers.

Spencer quickly became a Japanese All-Star, socking 36 homers in 1964 and

Shortstop Daryl Spencer hit 17 homers and 74 RBIs in 1958.
Brace Photo

38 home runs in 1965. He played three more years in Japan, retired after the 1968 season, and then came back as a player-coach for the 1971 and 1972 seasons.

"I did so well over there. I couldn't walk down the street without everyone recognizing me," said Spencer, now in his mid-80s. "I signed a lot of autographs."

Spencer, a Wichita, Kansas native, signed his first baseball contract in 1949 to play for an independent minor league team in Pauls Valley, Oklahoma. That year, Spencer, a right-handed hitter, raised eyebrows as he slammed 23 home runs to break the league record. Giants Hall of Fame pitcher Carl Hubbell scouted Spencer for one game, saw him hit a homer, and the next thing Spencer knew, the Giants purchased his contract from the Oklahoma team for $10,000 and five minor leaguers. He became a Giant farmhand.

"A crazy thing happened. In high school and semi-pro baseball, I never hit home runs, I was just a singles hitter. I hit maybe one home run in high school and none in legion ball," he said. "So I go professional and I hit 23 home runs. To this day, I can't explain it. I didn't have a coach that told me to try anything different. Boom, just like that, I became a home run hitter."

During his six seasons with the Giants, Spencer hit some memorable and record-breaking home runs. Spencer belted 17 home runs for the Giants in 1958, a record for San Francisco shortstops that held for four decades until Rich Aurilia broke it with 20 home runs in 1999.

He also hit the first home run in San Francisco Giants history, and the first home run on the West Coast in Major League history. Spencer crushed a Don Drysdale pitch over the left field fence in Seals Stadium as the Giants beat the Dodgers 8-0 on Opening Day on April 15, 1958 in front of 23,192 fans.

"That was quite a thrill," he said. "The San Francisco fans really welcomed us with open arms."

Spencer toiled in the Giants Minor League system for three years before making it to the Major Leagues in 1952 as a late season call-up. Spencer won a job with the Giants in 1953, hitting .208 and belting a major league career-best 20 home runs, as he split time at shortstop, third and second.

He lost the next two seasons to military service when he was drafted by the U.S. Army during the Korean War. Spencer, who was stationed in Oklahoma, wished he could have been part of the 1954 World Series championship team. "It was disappointing," he said.

But during the World Series, Spencer got a six-day furlough, hung out with his teammates in the clubhouse before the games, and then watched from the stands. Three weeks after the Giants swept the Indians, Spencer received a $2,000 check from the team. His teammates had voted to award him a share of the World Series money.

"I came back to visit, and I guess they felt sorry for me when I had to leave the team and go back to the Army," he said.

He returned to the team in 1957 as the team's starting shortstop. Despite a two-year layoff, Spencer hit a respectable .249 with 11 homers and 50 RBIs. He followed with two good seasons in San Francisco. Spencer enjoyed hitting in San Francisco because he hit better in cool weather than in hot weather. His best season was in 1958, when he hit .256 with 17 homers and a career-high 74 RBIs.

"I couldn't hit in hot weather. When I played in St. Louis and New York, it got real hot in the summer, but it never got that hot in San Francisco, so that's why I did good at Seals Stadium," Spencer said.

His favorite Giants highlight was in 1958 when he and Willie Mays hit two home runs each in back-to-back games against the Dodgers. In one of the games, Spencer drove in six runs, as he hit a double and triple to go with his two home runs. That year, with the Giants down by one run in the bottom of the ninth, Spencer hit a two-run, walk-off home run against the Cardinals to win 7-6. The next day, Spencer was the ninth inning hero again. The bases were loaded, and Spencer hit a swinging bunt down the third base line. Spencer beat the throw at first, allowing the winning run to score.

"He got a lot of key hits. He is remembered for being a really good clutch hitter," said Peter Magowan, the former Giants president who rooted for the team in his youth.

Former teammates said Spencer played and practiced hard. "Darryl was a tough, hard-nosed kind of player with good hustle," recalls former Giant second baseman Davey Williams, who retired in 1955 and coached the team for two years.

Williams, who pitched batting practice and helped run infield practices, among his many duties, remembers Spencer spent a lot of time working on his defense during Spring Training. "Daryl had me hit more groundballs than anyone else on the ball club. He wore me out," he said.

Spencer was traded to St. Louis in 1960 and four years later moved to Kobe, Japan, where he introduced his hard-nosed playing style to the Japanese players.

Spencer remembers vividly the moment he introduced the takeout slide at second base. It was the eighth inning of a scoreless tie, and Spencer walked with a runner on first base. When Spencer reached first base, he yelled out to the runner on second—fellow American Gordon Windhorn—and said, "If he hits a groundball, don't stop at third. I'm going to knock down the second baseman."

Sure enough, the hitter hit a grounder to the shortstop, and Spencer barreled down the basepath and slammed into the second baseman. "I knocked him out to left field, the ball fell out of his hands, and Windhorn scored," Spencer said.

The visiting team, along with its owner, argued on the field for 30 minutes, but the umpires ruled that Spencer did nothing wrong, and Spencer's team, the Braves, won 1-0. The Japanese players traditionally didn't slide into second base to attempt to break up double plays, Spencer said. Instead, they veered off to the right into the outfield, allowing infielders to throw to first unimpeded.

A few days later after the play at second, Spencer introduced the collision at the plate. He rounded third and crashed into the opposing team's catcher, knocking the ball out of his glove to score a run.

"The next thing I know, our players changed their whole style of base running," Spencer said. "They saw that we can win games by sliding hard, so the whole team started to slide hard."

Spencer, who played mostly second base, commuted by train to the Braves' ballpark in Nishinomiya, a city located between Kobe and Osaka in south central Japan. He always had an interpreter with him in the dugout. When he needed to communicate directly to teammates on the field during the game, he could. While he wasn't fluent in Japanese, many Japanese baseball terms are modeled after the way they are said in English. For example, "hitto" means "hit" and "raito" means right fielder, he said.

Spencer was one of the top sluggers in Japan in his first two years abroad, hitting 36 homers and 94 RBIs in 1964 and 38 home runs and 77 RBIs in 1965. But near the end of his second season, the Japanese players stopped throwing strikes to him to prevent him from beating a Japanese player for the home run title. One time, pitchers walked him eight straight times. Miffed, Spencer held the bat upside down at the plate once in protest.

"I feel sorry for Barry Bonds. He's in a different situation, but I really do understand how he feels," Spencer said.

Spencer was also known for crazy antics on the field, which endeared him to the fans. Once, he was in the original starting lineup, but right before the game, the manager gave him a day off. Spencer decided to go home. He took off his uniform and changed into a T-shirt and shorts. During the first inning, he walked into the dugout to fetch his bats before heading home.

Don Blasingame, an American coach for the Nankei Hawks, saw Spencer and yelled out, "Hey, where are you going? You're in the lineup."

Spencer looked at the scoreboard, which still listed him as the Braves' third hitter. That gave Spencer an idea.

"By the time I got to the dugout, the second batter was at home plate, so instead of going to my car, I walked to the on-deck circle in my T-shirt and shorts, swinging the bat and waiting for my turn at bat," he said. "I got fined $100, but the fans loved it."

Another time, Spencer was playing in Tokyo when he hit a routine ground ball. He ran hard down the first baseline, was called out, but he kept sprinting down the right field line and into the other team's bullpen in foul territory.

"Just for some dumb reason, I sat with the pitchers in the bullpen," he said.

After a few awkward moments, the game continued. "It was ball one, strike one, ball two, and the umpire calls time and yells, 'Get back to the dugout, Spencer.' I was talking to the Japanese pitchers in the bullpen," he recalled. "So I jogged back to the dugout, and the players are laughing and fans are going crazy."

Spencer extended his career by playing in Japan.
Photo by Matt Johanson

While other American players may have suffered from culture shock, Spencer thrived on the cultural differences. He remembers printing out business cards for himself when he realized the Japanese always handed out business cards after they introduced themselves to him.

"They start bowing and pass out their card to everyone. So I just said, 'Dammit, I'm going to get a card for myself,'" he said. "You know what I wrote on it? My card had no name or anything on it. I wrote 'My Card' on it."

Spencer retired after the 1968 season, but was lured back to Japan for the 1971 and 1972 seasons, where he was a player-coach at age 43 and 44. In his seven years in Japan, he batted .275 with 152 home runs and 391 RBIs.

Jim Albright, a Japanese baseball historian, said Spencer was Japan's best second baseman of the 1960s. "Only the brevity of his career kept him from having Japanese Hall of Fame-caliber accomplishment," he said.

Spencer, who in ten Major League seasons hit .244 with 105 homers and 428 RBIs, said he's not surprised so many Japanese players, from Hideo Nomo to Ichiro Suzuki, have performed so well in the United States.

"They had some great players when I played. Every team would have one or maybe two guys who could have played in America," he said.

Spencer is now enjoying retirement back in Wichita, where he lives with his wife. His two daughters live close by. The most strenuous thing he does nowadays, he said, is take care of his two grandchildren and do yard work.

He was elected into the Kansas Baseball Hall of Fame and the Wichita Sports Hall of Fame in 2004. During the induction ceremony in Wichita, his wife and two daughters presented him with a trophy.

Reflecting on his career, Spencer's first day in the big leagues was his most memorable moment.

"I had a pretty good career, but when people write and ask me what was my biggest moment, that was my biggest moment," Spencer said. "The Polo Grounds was shaped like an oval, and the entrance was in right field. I came through the gate and just sat there and looked at the Polo Grounds. I said, 'I made it. This is the big leagues and if I don't do anything else, my childhood dream came true.' And I wished my dad was here to see this. He wanted me to be a baseball player. I stood there for five minutes and tears came to my eyes."

His Japanese team, now called the Orix Blue Waves, occasionally invites him for ceremonies. He's also returned four times since the 1990s to take part in old-timers games. In 2002, he managed the American old-timers to one win and a tie in a two-game match against Japanese old-timers. He enjoys his trips back to Japan every time, Spencer said.

"Ballplayers don't want to admit it because they don't like to sign that many autographs when they're playing," he said. "But once you get out of the game, and no one is asking for your autograph, it's something you wish you can do again. When I visited in 2002, they asked me for my autograph, and I was really happy to sign for them."

MASANORI MURAKAMI

TRAILBLAZER

Delirious players poured out of the dugout when Team Japan recorded the final out. After reaching but losing the championship game the previous two years, the Japanese were primed to celebrate their victory of Women's World Series III in 2003. The euphoric world champions danced on the field in Gold Coast, Australia, and the gala lasted late into the night.

Japan's 4-1 win over Australia was especially sweet for manager Masanori "Mashi" Murakami, under pressure to produce a championship after bad play derailed his favored team the previous two years. "We were very happy because we lost the first two on errors and bonehead plays," said Murakami. "It felt very good to finally win."

After Murakami became the first Japanese player in the Major Leagues as a Giants pitcher in 1964 and 1965, he pitched 17 more years in the Japanese majors. Following his retirement at age 38, Murakami became a successful baseball broadcaster and writer and took the reins of Japan's top women's team in 2001.

When Murakami arrived at the Giants' Minor League affiliate in Fresno in 1964, the southpaw brought a big curveball, sharp control, and little command of English. Though he studied the language at Hosei Dai-Ni High School, Murakami made a greater effort in baseball, signing a professional contract with the Nankai Hawks when he was 17.

"First I thought I'd like to go to college, but the team's manager came to my house," Murakami said. "He said if I signed a contract, he wanted me to study baseball in America. I promised him I would."

Murakami played a year with the Hawks' Minor League team and then joined the Giants organization at age 19. After a year of demanding practices in a Japanese system designed to produce stars quickly, Murakami found his Giants workouts "very easy" in comparison.

*Pitcher Masanori Murakami became the first Japanese
player in the major leagues in 1964.*
© S.F. Giants

"Sometimes practice was like nothing," Murakami said. "I told the manager I wanted to throw. He said, 'No, no, no, today we'll just do conditioning.'"

Murakami won the California League Rookie of the Year award with an 11-7 record, good enough for a September call-up to the big club in San Francisco. There he struck out 15 and walked only one in nine relief appearances, compiling a 1.80 ERA.

The Giants liked Murakami enough to extend his contract, sparking a protest by the Hawks, who wanted him back. The teams reached a compromise that allowed the Giants to keep him another season, as long as the pitcher returned to the Hawks in 1966.

Murakami kept a Japanese-English dictionary in the dugout and communicated using his limited English skills and sign language. Once, his teammates taught him how to handle manager Herman Franks, and the next time Franks visited him on the mound, Murakami told his skipper, "Take a hike, Herman." Laughing, Franks left him in the game.

"Mashi" won the affection of his fellow Giants with his endearing personality; he bowed to his teammates when they made fine defensive plays behind him.

"Everybody took to him right away," said Tom Haller, former Giants catcher. "He was a nice kid and a good pitcher, a sidearm left hander with a very good breaking curveball."

He also proved popular with the Japanese-American community, especially after an episode at Dodger Stadium.

Murakami thought he had pitched strike three at the knees, but the umpire called a ball. Murakami walked off the mound and asked where it missed. The umpire shot back an answer that Murakami didn't understand. Then the frustrated pitcher threw his rosin bag 15 feet in the air. "It was the only time I complained," Murakami said.

Though the umpire nearly ejected him, catcher Jack Hiatt persuaded him to let Murakami off with a stern warning. But Murakami's small act of rebellion was a breath of fresh air to Japanese Americans who had lived in the country during and after World War II.

"A couple of days later, I was at a Japanese restaurant," he said. "An older Japanese man said, 'Hey, Mashi Murakami, nice to see you.' He was very happy. When the war started, Japanese [Americans] were sent to camps. After the war, they had nothing. They lost their homes and started with zero. Because of the war, they felt they couldn't say anything... But I'm from Japan and I didn't care. Baseball is just a game."

Murakami won four games and lost one in 1965, compiling a 3.75 ERA in 45 appearances. As agreed, he returned to Japan the following season, beginning a 17-year run for the Hawks, the Hanshin Tigers, and the Nippon Ham Fighters.

Pitching as a starter, reliever and closer, Murakami earned a 103-82 record with a 3.64 ERA in Japan. He appeared in Japan's All-Star Game in 1971 and in

*Murakami became a broadcaster, writer and
manager after his trans-Pacific pitching career.*
Photo by Matt Johanson

the Japan Series in 1966, 1973 and 1981.

After his retirement from the Japanese majors, Murakami tried to rejoin the Giants in the spring of 1983. Though almost 40 years old, he nearly made the team again.

Murakami's successful Japanese career in addition to his trailblazing outing to the United States made him a celebrity and a natural pick for the broadcast booth. Murakami became a commentator on Japanese and American baseball for Tokyo's NHK network, and a columnist for the *Nikkan Sports News.*

In 2001, Murakami became the manager of the Japanese national women's team in a new international league, competing against Canada, China, Hong Kong, South Korea, India, Australia, and the United States. A big part of his job was to convert his young players to hardball.

"In Japan, the women play softball or even with a rubber ball," he said. "In the first days of practice they learn very quickly."

Murakami served as the team's general manager in 2004, when Women's World Series IV came to the Japanese city of Uozu. Japan reached the championship game for the fourth straight year, setting up a rematch against the United States, the world champions of 2001.

Japan avenged its earlier loss to the Americans, winning its second-straight championship, 14-4. A record crowd of 10,000 wildly cheered the biggest blowout in the series' history.

"That was special because it was in Japan, and because no country had won two years in a row before," Murakami said.

Murakami continued to work in Japan as a baseball coach, scout, broadcaster, and writer. He and his wife, who have an adult son and daughter, live in Tokyo.

But "Mashi" also enjoys frequent visits to the United States and American ballparks. He's pleased to see Japanese players in ever-greater numbers, though he modestly denies any credit.

"None of them even know about me, because they weren't born yet," Murakami said. "For more than 30 years, no one else came. But I'm proud to see them now."

ORLANDO CEPEDA

"I Opened My Eyes"

Orlando Cepeda never expected the day to arrive. When he traveled to San Juan to attend the Giants' first-ever games in his native Puerto Rico, the national Museum of Sport unveiled a statue in his honor. Hiram Bithorn Stadium, where Cepeda played winter ball from 1962 to 1975, retired his number on the outfield wall. As Cepeda left the field, a Special Olympian gave him a medal she had won as a gift.

To a man Puerto Ricans vilified after his drug trafficking arrest in 1975, the events of May 23, 2004 were overwhelming.

"I never imagined things like this," said a teary Cepeda. "I got chills when I saw the statue."

The Giants' first baseman and outfielder from 1958 to 1966, Cepeda has experienced abysmal depths and dizzying heights in his days after baseball. He cleaned toilets and hauled garbage during a ten-month prison sentence, and he joined the Hall of Fame as one of the game's greatest players. Cepeda credits his Buddhist faith for turning his life around.

"The best thing that ever happened to me when I got in trouble in Puerto Rico. Because of that, I opened my eyes," Cepeda said. "I was introduced to Buddhism, and right now my life's better than ever."

The son of Puerto Rican baseball star Pedro "Perucho" Cepeda, Orlando grew up in a poor family that followed his father's career from city to city. Perucho, known as "the Bull" to his fans, was a shortstop who hit for both average and power, called by some the Babe Ruth of Puerto Rico. Negro League scouts pursued him, but Perucho never chose to confront the racism that a black, Spanish-speaking player would face in the United States. As a result, he never made more than $60 a week, and often gambled away his meager earnings.

Orlando, the "Baby Bull," began working out in 1953 with his father's old team, the Santurce Crabbers. There he played beside future Hall of Famers

Orlando Cepeda won Rookie of the Year honors in 1958.
Brace Photo

Roberto Clemente and Willie Mays, who joined the team for winter ball. Cepeda tried out for the New York Giants in 1955, when "beisbol" was the only word even close to English that he knew. The Giants signed the 17-year-old to a Minor League contract and paid him a $500 bonus.

Cepeda faced tough times as a black Minor League player in the segregated South of the 1950s, often unable to room in hotels or eat in restaurants with his teammates. Yet the alternative was tougher and less hopeful: most of his childhood friends became thieves, drug addicts, and even killers.

"I am a very lucky person to be born with the skills to play baseball," he said. "Through baseball I escaped from Puerto Rico, and I escaped poverty."

Cepeda reached the big club in 1958, the Giants' first year in San Francisco. He hit a home run on Opening Day at Seals Stadium, as the Giants shut out the Dodgers, 8-0. That day became Cepeda's favorite memory in a 17-year career that featured nine All-Star selections and three World Series appearances. Cepeda batted .312, clubbed 25 home runs, and hit 96 RBIs to win the Rookie of the Year award. San Francisco fans embraced him so warmly that even Mays was jealous, Cepeda said.

"When I started doing well, and they had me making headlines that Willie didn't make, maybe he took that very hard," Cepeda said.

Cepeda batted .308 and swatted 226 home runs during his Giants tenure, earning high rankings on the team's all-time lists for hits, doubles, home runs and runs. When the Giants fell behind the Dodgers in the finale of their three-game playoff in 1962, Cepeda drove in the tying run on the way to the Giants' eventual pennant-clinching win.

However, Cepeda faced adversity in several respects during his later Giants years. The team in 1959 brought up another superstar first baseman in Willie McCovey, and the two were forced to share playing time for many seasons. Cepeda later became embroiled in well-publicized disputes with manager Alvin Dark, who banned Spanish and Latin music from the clubhouse. The skipper also introduced a controversial plus-and-minus player evaluation system that indicated, incredulously, that Cepeda's overall performance hurt the team.

A knee injury ruined Cepeda's 1965 season, limiting him to just 33 games. After the team fired Dark, Cepeda quarreled with the new manager, Herman Franks, who wanted McCovey to start at first base.

Early in the 1966 campaign, the Giants traded Cepeda to the St. Louis Cardinals for left-handed pitcher Ray Sadecki. "I never thought Orlando would be traded. He was such a good player," said Giants teammate Jim Davenport. "It was unfortunate to have two great first basemen. I guess one of them was going to have to go. With Cepeda, we tried to get pitching. We didn't get back in return the value we gave up in Cepeda. No one wanted to see him leave."

The southpaw would pitch four years for the Giants, winning 32 games and losing 39. Cepeda was heartbroken by the decision, announced after a game on Mother's Day. But he blossomed in St. Louis, resuming his offensive production that eventually won him a place in Cooperstown.

Cepeda hit .301 and 20 homers as he won the Comeback Player of the Year award in 1966. The league's Most Valuable Player in 1967, Cepeda led the Cardinals to the pennant. Though Cepeda had a forgettable World Series, St. Louis won the championship over the Boston Red Sox. The Cardinals won another pennant in 1968.

Traded to the Atlanta Braves in 1969, Cepeda played a few more good years before knee problems hobbled him and his hitting declined. The American League's decision to allow designated hitters in 1973 afforded him a respectable season with the Red Sox. After batting .215 in 33 games for the Kansas City Royals, he retired in 1974.

During and after his baseball career, Cepeda made personal decisions he would later regret. He was unfaithful to his first and second wives, he revealed in his 1998 autobiography, *Baby Bull*. He also suffered from depression about the end of his career.

"You play baseball because you love it. But fame and celebrity can be seductive," he wrote. "For years we are cheered, and booed. The media courts us. The crowds roar. Then one day it's gone … For years after my career was over, when I watched a ballgame, I'd want to cry."

Then a decision during a visit to Colombia for a baseball clinic in 1975 led to serious legal problems. Cepeda agreed to carry five pounds of marijuana back to Puerto Rico for a friend. Police arrested him at the airport and charged him with smuggling 170 pounds of marijuana. The next three years leading to his trial and conviction were a torment. He became an outcast in Puerto Rico, where perfect strangers would insult and challenge him on the streets. Cepeda served his term at Eglin, a minimum-security prison in Ft. Walton, Florida, where he worked in the laundry room.

"From 1975 to 1978, it was a nightmare every single day," Cepeda said. "In fact, going to jail was a relief for me. Every day was a battle for me out on the street, and then I used to come home and take it out on my family."

Happiness eluded him after his release, as well. The Chicago White Sox hired him as a scout and batting coach in 1981, but quickly fired him. Cepeda was forced to sell some of his awards and trophies. After moving his family to Los Angeles in 1984, his second wife left him, returning to Puerto Rico with their sons. He admits that he considered suicide in these most difficult days.

Later, Cepeda became grateful for these hardships, which turned him down a path he otherwise might never have found.

"When you have everything, a big name and money, you think you don't need anything," he said. "When you hit the bottom hard like I did, you're ready to try something else. Fame and wealth and whatever can disappear in one second. That happened to me, and it was the best thing that ever happened to me."

Though raised a Catholic, Cepeda began exploring Buddhism, attending

Cepeda credits Buddhism for changing his life.
Photo by Matt Johanson

meetings and chanting every day. "That is what changed my life, 100 percent," he said. "Buddhism is a philosophy of life. It's a learning tool to change your life to really develop your potential as a human being. There's nothing abstract, nothing out there, there's no blind faith. Everything is black and white. I wish I practiced when I played ball. Buddhism is about common sense and wisdom and how to do the right thing at the right time. When you learn that, you don't get in trouble."

Cepeda's life improved quickly, starting with a lasting marriage to his third wife, Mirian Ortiz. Also Puerto Rican, Mirian would later provide recipes for the Latin dishes served at Orlando's Caribbean BBQ at the Giants' ballpark at 24 Willie Mays Plaza. Cepeda rejoined the Giants, helping scout and develop players in Mexico, the Dominican Republic, and other parts of Latin America. He also made community appearances for the team, visiting schools to tell students about the dangers of drugs and alcohol.

Cepeda received just 43 votes for the Hall of Fame in 1980, his first year of eligibility. After his return, the Giants campaigned hard for Cepeda's induction. In 1993, 250 voters supported him, 66 votes short of election. His final year on the baseball writers' ballot arrived in 1994, and Cepeda missed by seven votes.

But the "Baby Bull" would have his day. Though the writers denied him, the Hall's Veterans Committee elected him in 1999. He became just the second Puerto Rican in Cooperstown, joining the late Roberto Clemente. "I am proud to be a Puerto Rican," he said in his induction speech. "That is why this day is a wonderful day for Puerto Rico, for my family, and for all the Latin countries."

Cepeda's induction and words about his homeland helped mend his rift with other Puerto Ricans, but more important was his life and conduct since his prison sentence, he believes.

"Spanish people are very emotional people. They don't forget too easy," Cepeda said. "Anybody can make a mistake, but we have the opportunity to bounce back and show that we are good people."

MIKE McCORMICK

"THERE IS LIFE AFTER BASEBALL"

Since Mike McCormick won the Cy Young Award in 1967, Giants pitchers have earned two Hall of Fame inductions, seven 20-win seasons, and 36 All-Star selections.

But no other Giants pitcher won the Cy Young, bestowed every year upon the top pitcher in each league, for more than 40 years.

Fans who have long forgotten McCormick's wins, losses and injuries – and fans too young to have seen him play at all – still remember him for winning the prestigious award.

"All they remember are the good things about you, if you were any good," McCormick said. "I think you have to be a real detail-oriented fan to remember anything else."

McCormick pitched 11 of his 16 years for the Giants, compiling 107 wins and 96 losses for the team in New York and San Francisco. After his retirement from baseball, like most players of his era, McCormick pursued a different career, working briefly in securities and more than 20 years in office machines. "It took me a while, but I made the change," McCormick said. "There is life after baseball."

McCormick became a Giant straight out of high school, when the Giants' $50,000 bonus offer persuaded the southpaw to join the franchise instead of attending college. Under the rules at the time, players awarded such large bonuses could not go to the minors for two years.

"Mike was one of the early bonus rookies who had to stay with his Major League club as soon as he signed with the Giants," said Giants broadcaster Lon Simmons. "That made it tough."

Many of the early bonus rookies struggled for want of Minor League training, McCormick agreed. "It was not a good program for a lot of guys I saw on other teams," he said. "They would end up sitting on the bench for two years,

Pitcher Mike McCormick won the Cy Young Award in 1967.
© S.F. Giants

and then go to the minors for experience. My good fortune was that the Giants were old, making changes and preparing to come west. I got a chance to pitch enough to show them I could make the club."

A 17-year-old far from home, McCormick found New York a stark contrast from his hometown of Alhambra in Southern California. "I had never seen high-rise buildings that people lived in," he said. "They had as many people in six square blocks as we had in the whole town."

Prior to the club's move to San Francisco, McCormick played in the Giants' last two seasons at the Polo Grounds.

"I liked pitching there, though the ball carried pretty good to left and left center if you got it up in the air," he said. "It didn't carry well to right field. In that sense it was real similar to McCovey Cove. That short deck in right looks so appealing, but the crosswind knocks the ball down."

During McCormick's first six years with the Giants, he started 135 games, completed 44 of them and earned a 54-54 record. He became the youngest player to win 50 games. But McCormick also made 61 relief appearances, which he believes contributed to the shoulder problem he developed near the end of the 1961 campaign.

"In hindsight, you'd blame the manager for having you start and relieve," McCormick said. "I think the Giants did that a bit more than some teams. [Manager Bill] Rigney was tough on pitchers, but that wasn't uncommon. You had five good pitchers on some staffs, and the other guys were in the bullpen because they weren't good enough to start."

Doctors were never able to diagnose the exact nature of McCormick's shoulder problem, but it restricted him to 15 starts in the Giants' pennant-winning 1962 season. The team traded him to Baltimore prior to 1963.

"The Giants didn't have a clue what was wrong with me," McCormick said. "It may have been a bone spur or a rotator cuff. By today's standards, it would be a pretty simple surgery, but in those days, nobody wanted surgery. Very seldom did you see a pitcher rehab and come back and be effective."

Instead, McCormick changed his approach on the mound, substituting guile and control for raw power. "As a young kid, you challenge everybody," he said. "When you get older, you pitch more with your brain." After he pitched 216 innings with a 3.46 ERA for the Washington Senators in 1966, the Giants traded to get him back.

"Prior to having his arm hurt, Mike had a little more speed," recalled Tom Haller, the Giants catcher during most of McCormick's years with the team. After the injury, "Mike became a very good control pitcher, with a pretty good screwball that acted as a changeup for him."

McCormick's Cy Young season arrived in 1967, when he won 22 against 10 losses with a 2.85 ERA. He threw 14 complete games and struck out 150 batters.

© S.F. Giants

The Giants awarded McCormick a "gorgeous" ring in honor of his achievement. Yet McCormick believes that he pitched better in other years.

"There were a couple of years when I felt I pitched better or as well as the year I won the Cy Young," McCormick said. "You have to be lucky, also. In that year, if I needed the save, I got it. If I needed a defensive play made, I got it. If I needed a base hit to get me the run to win, I got it. As a pitcher, you can't control those things, but they make the difference between good and great."

McCormick retired from baseball following a back injury in 1971, turning to the business career he had started during his off-season winters. "I spent my last two off-seasons training to work in the securities business. I was starting to develop a client base the last year I played," he said.

McCormick bought and sold mutual funds and bonds for three years, long enough to realize that he wanted to do something else. "I never really liked it, but I liked what it taught me about my personality," he said. "I was much better one-on-one than working on the phone, dialing for dollars."

McCormick instead began a 27-year career in copiers and office machines, working for Ricoh and later Danka Office Imaging. He became Danka's regional director, responsible for the company's sales, service and administration "from Fresno to Alaska," and responsible for several hundred employees.

"It was a good career for me," McCormick said. "I made a good living, for myself and my family. It was a dog-eat-dog business, but I guess I did something right.

"Xerox was always the dominating company we all competed against," he said. "The technology was always changing. When I started, I was in the copier business. When I retired, it was the digital printing business. A critical part of the business was the technical service you provide."

McCormick has kept active as a Giants alumnus, occasionally broadcasting games, assisting in Spring Training, and appearing at fantasy camps. Pitching a few innings at a fantasy event in 2003, McCormick became the only Giants pitcher to play in the team's last four ballparks: 24 Willie Mays Plaza, Candlestick Park, Seals Stadium, and the Polo Grounds.

"You get a mixed bag," McCormick said of the fantasy events. "There are women and children mixed in with it. It's evident that some people have never played baseball before. Some of the younger guys are still playing, and want to see how far they can hit it. I always tell them, 'It's not my fantasy, it's yours.' I can't throw the ball hard anymore, but if I throw a curve, none of them can hit it.

They're out there to have a good time, so I throw it down the middle. Most of them get a different appreciation about the size of the park."

McCormick retired from Danka in 2002. He moved with his wife Dierdre and their teenage daughter to Pinehurst, North Carolina, "world famous for its golf."

McCormick jogs and plays golf "on every day ending in Y," except Sunday. The pace of life is much slower there, McCormick says, and he likes the atmosphere and the climate.

"You can't beat how and where we're living," he said, "though I do miss the Bay Area. I think what I miss there are my family and the Giants."

Would anything be different if he hadn't won the Cy Young?

"That's an interesting question," McCormick said. "I don't think financially things would've been any different, with no agents and the way we were compensated. Maybe that would have made some difference in terms of fan recogni-

McCormick pursued a second career in office machines.
Photo by Matt Johanson

tion and my part in the Giants family."

One could forgive McCormick for wanting to keep that exclusive honor, but he rooted for Giants starter Tim Lincecum, who won the award in 2008 and 2009, andGiants starter Jason Schmidt, when he contended for the award in 2003 and 2004.

"[The distinction] is nice, but at the same time, somebody else has got to win it sometime," McCormick said.

JIM DAVENPORT

COMPANY MAN

W hen Giants management has a major need or a vacant position to fill, it turns to Jim Davenport, a former San Francisco third baseman and manager who's worked for the club for more than 40 years.

In 1995, after the Giants fired their Triple-A manager in midseason, Davenport took over the team for the rest of the year. The following year, he served as a first base coach for the big league club under manager Dusty Baker. He's even worked as a scout, surveying upcoming Giants opponents and writing detailed reports to the team.

Now, the Giants entrust their minor leaguers, particularly their infielders, into the capable hands of the 1962 Gold Glove winner. As special assistant of player personnel, Davenport is a minor league roving instructor. He coaches youngsters to improve their defensive skills and has helped the likes of Bill Mueller and Pedro Feliz as they climbed their way up to the major leagues.

"It's great to be in the big leagues working with the big league players, but I think you get a lot more satisfaction working with a minor league kid and seeing him progress from day to day," said Davenport, now in his late 70s.

"Davvy" coaches minor leaguers in Arizona during Spring Training, then works with the Giants' Minor League clubs during the season. He primarily focuses on the Single-A San Jose Giants and the Triple-A Fresno Grizzlies, but during the 2004 season, he spent some time with the Single-A Hagerstown Suns in Maryland.

Davenport serves as a troubleshooter for Giants' general manager Brian Sabean, said former team President Peter Magowan. If Sabean needs Davenport to coach young infielders, from fielding the ball to footwork around the bases, Sabean sends Davenport to those teams.

"Brian will say, 'Go on out to Hagerstown. We need you to work with this third baseman or shortstop.' He does whatever Brian wants him to do,"

Third baseman Jim Davenport won a Gold Glove in 1962.
© S.F. Giants

Magowan said. "He loves working with young kids. He's been around so long that he's just got a lot of wisdom about the game of baseball."

Born in Siluria, Alabama, a small rural town, Davenport was a star high school quarterback who received a scholarship to attend the University of Southern Mississippi. During college in the summer of 1955, he was playing semi-pro baseball when a Giants scout saw him and offered him a Minor League contract. Davenport signed with the Giants, and three years later, he became the starting third baseman for the Giants during the team's first season in San Francisco in 1958.

Davenport was the leadoff hitter in the first game ever at Seals Stadium and struck out in his first at-bat against Dodgers starter Don Drysdale. In his second at-bat, he hit a single for his first Major League hit. That year, he finished the season batting .256 with 12 home runs and 41 RBIs, and led the National League with 17 sacrifice hits.

He hit decently, but made his mark with his glove, leading all National League third basemen in fielding percentage from 1959 to 1961 and becoming an All-Star and Gold Glove winner in 1962. Years later, during the 1967 and 1968 seasons, he set a National League record by playing 97 straight games without an error at third base.

"Brooks Robinson was probably a better hitter, but I didn't think he was a better defensive player than Jimmy. He could play with anybody," said former Giants pitcher Mike McCormick.

Davenport, who played all his 13 years as a Giant, batted .258 with 77 home runs and 456 RBIs in his career. His best offensive season was his All-Star year of '62, when he batted .297 with a career-high 14 homers and 58 RBIs. He played a key role in the Giants winning the pennant in '62 against the Dodgers. It was the top of the ninth inning in the deciding game of a three-game playoff against Los Angeles. With the bases loaded and the score tied, Davenport walked to drive in the eventual winning run.

Davenport, who later played other infield and outfield positions, retired in 1970 at age 36. "I was never a great ballplayer, but I was fortunate to spend that many years that I did with the ball club. I played with some awful great players," said Davenport, referring to players like Willie Mays, Willie McCovey and Orlando Cepeda. "I was fortunate to play in one All-Star game and one World Series. A lot of guys don't get a chance to do that."

Davenport, voted by fans in 1982 as the third baseman on the Giants' 25th Anniversary Dream Team, liked Seals Stadium and admits Candlestick Park was tough to play in, but the alternative was far worse. "It was either play there or go back to the minor leagues," he said.

After retiring, Davenport managed Triple-A Phoenix for the Giants from 1971 to 1973, then left the Giants to coach the San Diego Padres from '74 to '75. He then returned to the Giants as a coach from 1976 to 1982.

Former Giant Dave Heaverlo said Davenport was a unique coach at the time because he cared and became close to players during an era when the front offices in baseball didn't encourage friendships between management and the team. "He always had a smile and a handshake and was generally concerned with us as people," Heaverlo said.

After serving as an advanced scout in '83 and '84, Davenport got his wish when he was hired to manage the Giants in 1985. The season, however, became a disaster, as the Giants finished 62-100, 33 games out of first place. The hitting was dismal as the Giants ranked last in batting with a .233 average, last in hits and runs scored, and next to last in runs batted in. Owner Bob Lurie fired Davenport near the end of the season when the Giants were 56-88.

"Davvy unfortunately got stuck with not a very good team, and because of that, he never lasted through the year," said Giants broadcaster and former second baseman Duane Kuiper. "But you know what? There isn't a nicer guy than Jim Davenport. He'd be the first guy I would want to have a drink with at the bar."

Davenport's pleasant personality may actually have worked against him as a skipper, McCormick believes. "The worst thing that could have happened to him was making him a Major League manager," he said. "The players knew he was a nice, soft guy. They just took advantage of him. He really had no control."

Davenport disputes that notion. "I don't think they walked over me that year. I won't buy that," said Davenport, who added that McCormick wasn't part of the team that year. He doesn't blame the players, but also wishes he had a better team. Injuries to the pitching staff contributed to the teams woes, he added.

"When you have a chance to manage, you have to jump at it," he said. "I'm glad I got the chance."

After the Giants banished him, Davenport spent the next six seasons with other clubs, coaching third base for Philadelphia and Cleveland for two years each, then serving as an advanced scout for the Tigers for two years. Davenport reunited with the Giants in 1993, coaching the Single-A San Jose Giants until 1995. That year, he took over the Triple-A Phoenix Firebirds when the Giants fired the manager in mid-season.

The Giants asked Davenport to manage its Triple-A ballclub again in 1998 for the team's inaugural year in Fresno. Davenport led the team to the Pacific Coast League Southern Division championship that year. Since then, Davenport has served as a roving Minor League instructor and special assignment scout for Sabean.

Magowan, who brought Davenport back to the club in 1993, said Davenport exemplifies the type of long-term relationships the Giants build with their former players.

"Everyone in baseball likes Jimmy Davenport. He's sort of quiet. He's got a nice sense of humor. He's very loyal to the organization," Magowan said. "He's the kind of example we like to show young players. Here is someone who's been

*Davenport worked throughout the Giants
organization as a scout, coach and manager.*
Photo by Matt Johanson

a Giant for 40 years or more. They take care of us. We take care of them. We have that kind of relationship with Jimmy."

Even when Davenport was a player, he worked in different roles for the Giants. For several off-seasons, Davenport, McCormick, and former catcher Tom Haller worked in the Giants public relations office, attending functions and going to lunch with season ticket holders.

Davenport, who lives in San Carlos with his wife Betty, works with Giants Minor Leaguers during Spring Training and throughout the season. He helps the young players focus on the fundamentals of fielding, but also talks to them about life in baseball.

"Keep working, working, working is my theory. Just keep working and you will get better," Davenport said. "And I talk baseball. Sometimes you just sit and talk out on the field about what it takes. That there will be certain ups and downs in baseball. You have to tell the kids how to handle the down part."

Bill Mueller was Davenport's most prized pupil. The Giants third baseman from 1996 to 2000, Mueller consistently hit around .300 while playing for San Francisco. After joining the Boston Red Sox, he won the American League batting championship in 2003 with a .326 average.

"He was a hard worker and wanted to learn and make himself better," Davenport said. "He was just dedicated to just taking care of stuff on and off the field."

Former Giants infielder Cody Ransom raves about Davenport, who coached him for a few weeks at Single-A Bakersfield in 1999. "He has a lot of wisdom. He's easy to talk to and doesn't try to push things on you," he said. "He just gives you pointers here and there."

Davenport, who has five children, plans to be a Giant forever.

"I feel like I can contribute. And as long as I feel good, I enjoy doing it," he said. "I love the Giants."

GAYLORD PERRY

THE SPITTERS AND THE SKIPPER

Gaylord Perry still guards his secrets. Ask the "Great Expectorator" today about his "special" pitch—what he used on the ball, or where he hid his supply of it —and the longtime Giants hurler may simply say, "I don't remember."

But Perry's association with the spitball will be hard to live down. When Perry visited the White House in 1970, the first thing President Nixon asked him was where he hid his grease: "Gaylord, tell me, where do you get it?" Fans ask him to sign jars of Vaseline at card shows. Broadcaster Lon Simmons once introduced Perry as the pitcher who made hitters "so mad they could spit."

In an unusual act of candor, Perry himself revealed much of his wet craft in his 1974 autobiography, *Me and the Spitter*. In the book, Perry admitted to throwing mud balls, sweat balls, Vaseline balls, and K-Y vaginal jelly balls.

"I reckon I tried everything but salt and pepper and chocolate sauce," he wrote.

Perry would become the first pitcher to win the Cy Young Award in both leagues, and was elected to the Baseball Hall of Fame in 1991. After his retirement, he built a baseball program from the ground up at a small North Carolina college. But Perry's post-Giants years also included hardship and tragedy: a bankruptcy that cost him his farm and the automobile accident that killed his wife.

❈ ❈ ❈ ❈ ❈ ❈ ❈

Perry learned his baseball at a young age on the North Carolina tobacco farm where he was raised.

"I first started playing ball in the cow pasture with my dad who would play with [my brother] Jim and me every chance he got," Perry said. "I remember our neighbor saying, 'All those Perry boys want to do is play baseball, and their dad is even worse.'"

Pitcher Gaylord Perry won 134 games in 10 years as a Giant.
© S.F. Giants

Perry signed with the Giants in 1958 and debuted in the majors in 1962, winning three and losing one in 13 appearances. But his breakthrough year was 1964, when Perry won 12 and lost 11, pitching 206 innings with 105 strikeouts. As chance would have it, 1964 was also the year Perry admitted to first throwing the spitball.

"I was the only pitcher left in the bullpen in a double header against the New York Mets. The sucker game lasted 23 innings," Perry recalled. "When I got to the mound to start the 13th inning, my catcher Tom Haller says, 'Kid, it's time to put something on the ball...' We made a triple play, and a few double plays. Del Crandall pinch hit for me in the 23rd inning and got a base hit to score Jim Davenport. That's what I needed to get started."

Perry's antics infuriated managers such as Casey Stengel, Billy Martin, Whitey Herzog, and Sparky Anderson, and players Pete Rose and Hank Aaron.

During his first wet years, "I had to use gobs of stuff. I put it on my cap, my pants, my shirt, underneath the tongue of my shoe and on my belt," he wrote in his autobiography. "I always had it in at least two places, in case the umpires would ask me to wipe off one. I never wanted to be caught out there without anything. It wouldn't be professional."

But the umpires never caught Perry in the act during his Giants years, nor for many years afterwards, as he learned to deliver the wet pitch with a smaller load.

"He had ways of going about what he had to do to get the job done," Tom Haller, the Giants' catcher from 1961 to 1967, cryptically said.

While greasing a ball is illegal, there's no rule against tricking the batter into expecting a spitball. Perry took full advantage, touching his hand to his hat, neck, ear, face or shirt prior to delivering the ball. Bewildered and infuriated batters swung low for the spitter, only to miss the dry pitches that crossed the plate belt-high.

"Gaylord also threw the forkball, similar to today's split-finger pitch. A wet pitch would have a similar spin on the ball," Haller said. "It became a brain game. A lot of guys would anticipate certain things and not get them, which worked to his advantage."

Nor is there any regulation prohibiting pitchers from planting doubt in batters' minds through other means, like leaving Vaseline or K-Y jelly around the clubhouse or training room.

John D'Acquisto, another former Giants pitcher and teammate of Perry, recalled an especially provocative example involving Chicago Cubs manager Herman Franks, who had once been Perry's manager with the Giants.

"I saw him do this," said D'Acquisto. "He's got a tube of Vaseline, and he squirted it all over the ball. Herman Franks was the one who taught him how to throw that damn pitch, OK? He's covered the ball up with Vaseline. He took the ball, rolled it up to Herman Franks and hit him right in the foot.

"Herman went nuts! He tried to pick up the ball and he couldn't pick it up," D'Acquisto said. "We were dying laughing. He started yelling at the umpires, and he almost got run out of the game before the game even got started. 'He's going to throw spitballs all game long. He's taunting us. Look at this BS!' And Gaylord goes, 'No, it's a forkball, it's a forkball!' Forkball my butt," D'Acquisto said.

There was more to Perry's game than Vaseline and grease. Also important was his fiercely competitive nature, as Simmons recalled.

"Nobody likes to lose, but it just drove Gaylord crazy," Simmons said. "One time in Houston, he gave up a walk-off base hit. Nellie Fox got an infield hit to win the ballgame and beat Perry. Perry came walking off the mound to dugout, and he picked up Fox's bat and broke it. Then the league made Perry pay for the bat. That's the way he was about losing ballgames."

Perry won 134 and lost 109 in 10 seasons as a Giant, striking out 1,606 and once no-hitting the Cardinals. He led the league in innings pitched (328.2), shutouts (5) and wins (23) in 1970.

Yet the Giants traded him to the Cleveland Indians for southpaw Sam McDowell in 1971. The move saved the Giants money, but cost the team dearly in every other way. While Perry would win two Cy Young awards and 180 games for seven teams during the next 12 years, McDowell won 11 and lost 10 in the next two years as a Giant.

"I absolutely wanted to stay," Perry said. "I had a home there, and kids in school. I loved it. It wasn't my idea to get traded. [Former Giants owner] Horace Stoneham was a great guy, but at the time they were having financial troubles, like a lot of clubs have right now. They had to make decisions."

❖ ❖ ❖ ❖ ❖ ❖ ❖

The Cleveland Indians won 60 games and lost 102 the year before Perry arrived. The tall right-hander helped the club improve to 72-84 in a shortened 1972 season.

"When I got to Cleveland, I looked in center field and Willie [Mays] wasn't there," Perry said. "I knew I was in trouble."

The club finished far out of the pennant race, but Perry won 24 against 16 losses, earning his first Cy Young Award. Perry won games for losing teams for most of his remaining years, constantly aggravating opponents but always passing umpires' inspections. How could he not? They took a moment to walk 60 feet and 6 inches from the plate to the mound, and he only needed an instant to wipe away his substance of the day.

Where he hid his supply was a question of constant conjecture. Opponents filmed him from multiple positions trying to unravel his system. Perry himself fueled the fire with his book and his shenanigans. Even his four-year-old daughter Allison contributed to the mystique.

"Allison, when she was a little girl, would find the writers and would slip to them and say, 'I know where my dad hides the stuff,'" Perry recalled. Where, the excited writers asked her, where did her dad hide his grease? "He hides it in his garage," the girl would tell them.

Perry joined the San Diego Padres from 1978 to 1979. "What a great place to play baseball," he said. "There I only had to pitch about seven innings of every game I started. This is the first time that I had a guy named Rollie Fingers. He came in and helped me win the Cy Young Award that year."

Not until 1982 did the umpires finally eject him for the first and only time, when he pitched for the Seattle Mariners against the Boston Red Sox. Umpire Dave Phillips warned Perry in the fifth inning, then ejected him in the seventh for throwing an illegal pitch. Perry later took a polygraph test to prove his innocence, but the league nonetheless suspended him for ten games.

The "pine tar" incident brought Perry back into the umpires' gun-sights in 1983, after Perry had joined the Kansas City Royals. After teammate George Brett hit a ninth-inning homer to take the lead over New York, Yankees manager Billy Martin protested that Brett had broken the rules by using a bat with too much pine tar. The umpires agreed, calling Brett out to apparently end the game. It was unprecedented: Brett had hit a game-losing home run.

In the pandemonium that followed, Perry grabbed Brett's bat and headed for the clubhouse, only to be stopped by stadium security. Perry, too, was ejected and later fined $250. American League President Lee MacPhail later overturned the umpires' decision because Brett had not violated "the spirit of the rules."

The Royals prevailed when the teams resumed the game the following month. When Perry retired in 1983 at the age of 45, he had amassed 314 wins against 265 losses, winning 20 games in a season five times. He struck out 3,534 batters and compiled a lifetime ERA of 3.10.

❉❉❉❉❉❉❉

Perry returned to his North Carolina farming roots after retirement, growing tobacco, peanuts, corn and soybeans. But his 410-acre ranch in Martin County proved unprofitable during the US grain embargo against the USSR, President Carter's attempt to punish the Soviets for invading Afghanistan.

"Farming got tougher, and it's even tougher now," Perry said. "I don't see how you can make it, unless you've got the farm paid for, equipment paid for, and money in the bank. The grain embargo really hurt us. You can't hardly give it away."

Perry was forced to declare bankruptcy and give up the farm in 1986. But a new opportunity presented itself that year. Limestone College, a private university of 300 students in Gaffney, South Carolina, contacted Perry about starting a baseball program.

"We needed to beef up our enrollment, and we were talking about adding athletic teams to attract students," said Craig Drennon, then Limestone's athletic director. "We had no baseball field at all, but we were looking to get 20 or 25 kids to play. I noticed an article about Gaylord being back in North Carolina, working his peanut farm, so I picked up the phone and called.

"He didn't even know where we were, but he and his wife Blanche stopped by," said Drennon. "Gaylord was so engaged, such a down-home type of person, and Blanche was the same way. I could tell he was interested, and we started talking about possibilities. We offered him a three-year deal, and he said, 'I ain't had contract more than a year since I can't remember. The last contract I had was 30 days.'"

Closing the deal took a little time, prompting Limestone's Director of Communications Andy Solomon to feed the press a delicious quote: "The reason why it took us so long to sign Gaylord was that the pen kept slipping out of his hand." Eventually Perry did sign, bought a home in Gaffney and set to work building a program.

"His name alone had kids coming from all over the country," said Dennis Bloomer, coach of Limestone's softball team at the time, and later of women's basketball.

"We had some great years," said Drennon. "We gave him five scholarships. At the time, it cost $10,000 a year to go Limestone. So we put up $50,000, and I think we paid him $30,000. We didn't have much invested in it. But Gaylord attracted 40-45 students the first year to play for him. We had kids come from Canada, California, Texas, everywhere. The truth is, the program brought us in a bunch of money. It was a great move on our part."

Before Perry could field a team, he had to build the field. Prior to his arrival, Limestone had only an empty patch of dirt where Bob Prevatte Field now stands.

"He had an opportunity to build the park like he wanted to build it," Drennon said. "He did it himself and he built a pitcher's park. You have to knock the hell out of the ball to get it out of there."

From home plate to the foul poles is 325 feet, farther than home to the right field pole at Pacific Bell Park. The alleys are 375 feet deep, and 390 feet separate the plate from dead center.

"Gaylord was able to squeeze every foot out of the site," said Anthony Lombardo, Perry's successor as Limestone's baseball coach. "It is indeed a pitcher's park, because there is no carry to the ball from left center to the right field foul pole.

"Also, as ballparks go, there is some room between the foul lines and the fence, which does indeed help the pitchers," Lombardo said. "Some of those foul balls stay in play for easy outs."

More than once, Drennon said, Perry's players asked him to teach them his special pitch. "They asked him all the time," Drennon laughed. "He'd laugh and tell stories about it, like the time he shook hands with Reggie Jackson with

Perry signs autographs at a Giants' fan fest.
Photo by Matt Johanson

Vaseline all over his hands before a ballgame. I don't think he ever taught them how to throw it, though."

When sportswriters asked Perry about teaching the spitter, he always gave them the same answer, Solomon said.

"He would say, 'No, I teach a similar pitch called the split-finger fastball,' and he would wink when he said that," Solomon said. "In all honesty, none of our pitchers were capable of controlling a spitter, and some couldn't even control a splitter."

None of the Limestone Saints approached Perry's big league success, but one signed a professional contract.

"I liked the coaching fine," Perry said, "but the fundraising got ridiculous."

Some of the players overestimated their talent, Perry said. "All of them [college players] thought they were going to get signed to play pro ball," he said. "When they saw the competition, they'd change their minds right quick. It's a big step."

Tragedy also visited Perry's life during his years at Limestone. In September 1987, his wife Blanche flew to Florida to join their daughter, who had just given birth to a baby girl. A 67-year-old driver impaired by his medication ran a stop sign and plowed into Blanche's Chevrolet on U.S. Highway 27 near Lake Wales. The elderly man survived, but Blanche perished. A family celebration instantly became a family calamity.

"Gaylord would always pitch batting practice, and Blanche would shag baseballs in the outfield," said Drennon. "They had an unbelievable relationship, and it all came to an end within minutes."

"I always counted on her being there," Gaylord Perry told jurors in the civil trial he brought against the driver in 1989. "It didn't matter if I won or lost, she always knew the right thing to say at the right time." Before jurors could decide the case, the trial attorneys agreed on a settlement that compensated Perry with $1 million.

❀ ❀ ❀ ❀ ❀ ❀ ❀

Perry returned to Limestone, leading the Saints to a 58-45 record and two NAIA District Six playoffs in his first four seasons.

Cooperstown summoned Perry in 1991, as the baseball writers elected Perry on his third ballot appearance. He chose a San Francisco Giants cap for his Hall of Fame plaque, and spoke warmly of his first big league team in his induction speech.

"My years in San Francisco gave me a chance to play with some of the greatest," Perry told the audience. "I looked over at first base, and there was the great Willie McCovey. I had to follow in the pitching rotation the great Juan Marichal ... and then [there was] the greatest player that I saw, Willie Mays. I played with these guys for ten years."

Perry's speech also recognized his late father and wife. "The most special people in the world who helped me over these years are my family and very close friends," Perry said. "A few of the people that played a great part also are not with us any longer ... My dad, boy, he would love this day, that's for sure, and one who was just very special, Blanche, the dear and special lady who supported me 100 percent over the years and was the mother of my children."

But Perry also pleased the crowd with a few lighthearted quips about his special pitches, his covert substances, and all the umpires who failed to find them.

"Of course you know it wouldn't be fitting if I didn't say a few words about those umpires," Perry said. "I really knew them by their first names. We seemed to have a lot of business up there on the mound." The audience shook with laughter as Perry told them, "My catchers were the ones that called all those pitches."

Perry's Hall of Fame plaque does not mention his spitters, but does commend him for "playing mind games with hitters through array of rituals on the mound."

Perry's induction caused some controversy, though, and not only among the hitters he faced. Former Giants pitcher John Montefusco, for one, was angry about Perry's antics. "We all knew that Gaylord was cheating, but there was nothing we could do about it," Montefusco said. "A lot of people don't think he belongs in the Hall of Fame for that reason."

Nevertheless, South Carolina's Legislature honored Perry's achievements by declaring Jan. 17, 1991 "Gaylord Perry Day" in the state.

"Perry has been more than a baseball coach," the legislators wrote. "He works hard to teach his boys proper character traits and build them into men. He emphasizes academics as a priority and graduation as a goal."

Perry coached one more year at Limestone before walking away from the program he created and the campus buildings he helped to restore.

Perry later remarried. He and his wife enjoy traveling, fishing and their ranch in the North Carolina mountains. Perry makes appearances, signs autographs and still returns reporters' phone calls. For some reason, they often call after some ballplayer gets caught cheating.

After Sammy Sosa broke a corked bat in a 2003 game, earning him an ejection and a suspension, Perry's phone rang all day. The "Great Expectorator" cheerfully shared the advice he offered the embattled Cubs' slugger.

"I told him to get a better carpenter," Perry said.

WILLIE MAYS

THE GODFATHER

Willie Mays had already made a fair contribution, but he found another way to help the Giants by filling a role no one else could. Mays became a mentor, coach and friend to slugger Barry Bonds, especially after his father Bobby Bonds died in 2003.

Bonds broke into tears when he stepped into the batting cage in his first off-season without his father. He called in his godfather Mays to supervise some of his workouts. Then when Bonds matched and passed Mays' career mark of 660 home runs in April 2004, the "Say Hey Kid" passed him a torch, literally and figuratively.

"I don't feel I'm ahead of Willie because Willie is my mentor," Bonds said. "He always will be. I still feel he's the greatest player of all time. That hasn't changed."

Bonds also expressed relief at accomplishing a feat worthy of his godfather's approval, but Mays said he doesn't have to worry about that.

"Barry doesn't need approval from me because I've been there since he was five years old," Mays said. "Whatever he does, right or wrong, I'm going to be there for him. I think it's appropriate that he does it in a Giants uniform. That's what I really wanted."

Mays spent 21 years in his Giants uniform, though his opening 0-for-13 drought in his rookie year made him doubt his future in baseball. Manager Leo Durocher tried to put his mind at ease. "Son, as long as I'm manager of this particular ballclub, you are my center fielder," he said. The next day, Mays hit a home run off Hall of Famer Warren Spahn.

The "Say Hey Kid" went on to break the Giants' career records in nearly every offensive category, even though he played his first years in the Negro Leagues, lost two years to the Korean War, and spent his final two years with the New York Mets. He played in four World Series, including the Giants' sweep of

Center fielder Willie Mays was a 20-time All-Star.
© S.F. Giants

© S.F. Giants

the Cleveland Indians in 1954, and appeared in a record 24 All-Star games.

"The greatest thing about Mays was his anticipation," said Giants broadcaster Lon Simmons. "If the ball was out on the dirt away from the catcher, Mays moved up a base. Watch a game today, and watch a ball get by the catcher, and watch when the runner moves. I guarantee you that ball will be halfway to the backstop by the time the runner moves. Mays ran before the ball hit the ground, because he knew it was going to hit the ground."

Mays' astonishing catch in the 1954 World Series and his four-homer game against Milwaukee in 1960 rank among his most famous highlights, but he contributed to the team in many other ways. For instance, Mays tried to moderate the heavy drinking of third baseman Jim Ray Hart, and sometimes donated his $100 post-game interview money to four lower-earning teammates, $25 apiece.

"If you watched Mays play, every day was a highlight even if he went 0-for-4, because he did something," said Simmons. "Willie could play an entire game or an entire week and not have a highlight, specifically, but by God you noticed him all the time when he was there. He didn't have to do something great.

"Barry is a better hitter than Willie was, I think," Simmons added. "But Mays was at the top in hitting, in fielding, in running, in thinking, in controlling the ball game."

Mays was the first to combine power and speed, with 338 stolen bases. He was a lifetime .302 batter who recorded an all-time record 7,095 putouts in the outfield.

"My game wasn't home runs. I was a guy who tried to do everything," Mays said. "I was a good base runner. I could throw and field. I wasn't one-dimensional. I played as long as I could and I enjoyed every minute."

Actually, Mays didn't enjoy learning the Giants traded him to the Mets in 1972, though the move proved a homecoming of sorts for the star who had already played six years in New York.

After he retired in 1973, Mays took a front office job with the Mets. He also worked in public relations for various companies, including Colgate and Bally's Resorts. After a lifetime in baseball, getting by in business took some adjustments, he wrote in his 1988 autobiography, *Say Hey*.

"I understood, roughly, about keeping appointments. But in business, when they say eleven o'clock, they mean eleven o'clock, not 11:05," Mays wrote. "It took me three or four years, but I grew up in learning what the business world was about. I think I'm as comfortable now in the business world as I once was in baseball."

The Bally's job actually led to Mays' shocking banishment from baseball shortly after he entered the Hall of Fame in 1979. Mays' position involved public appearances and golf outings with high-rollers from Bally's Atlantic City casino, and former baseball commissioner Bowie Kuhn objected to the connection with gambling. When Kuhn forced Mays to choose between Bally's and baseball, Mays gave up his Mets job.

"That never should have happened. It was a dumb move by the commissioner," said former Giants President Peter Magowan.

While at Bally's, Mays created the Say Hey Foundation, a charity that financially supports needy children with their education expenses.

Commissioner Peter Ueberroth overturned his ban in 1985. General manager Al Rosen brought Mays to the Giants' front office in 1986, where he's been ever since. Magowan gave Mays a lifetime contract when he and other investors bought the team in 1992.

Mays lives with his wife Mae in Atherton. He has one adopted son from his first marriage. Now in his eighties, Mays underwent hip replacement surgery in 2004.

"He always goes to Spring Training," said Magowan. "He does a fair amount of speaking engagements for the Giants. He also talks to players, maybe not so much on the field anymore because his eyesight is not what it once was."

Mays visited the Giants clubhouse often after Bobby Bonds died, to support his godson who as a child played beside Mays' locker at Candlestick Park.

The torch Mays gave Bonds was produced during San Francisco's unsuccessful bid to win the 2012 Olympic Games. Mays had diamonds mounted to form his number 24, Bonds' number 25, and a large 660 for the home run total they both reached.

Mays often appears with his godson, Barry Bonds.
Photo by Matt Johanson

"I just feel like right now I completed our family circle," Bonds said after his blast into McCovey Cove. "Willie took my dad under his wing when he first came up and taught my dad a lot about baseball and became a real close friend of my father's.

"It's my dad in right field, Willie in center field and I get to be in left field," Bonds said. "There's just no greater feeling than completing the circle of my family."

The godfather had the last word in an on-field ceremony later that week. By that time, Bonds had already hit number 661.

"It's not about Barry, and it's not about myself," he said. "It's all about history and the Giants. Can you find a better fellow to break a record like mine? I told him many times that I wish he would do it, because I know it's going to stay in the family."

JUAN MARICHAL

"Like Picasso"

A capacity crowd at Santo Domingo's Olympic Stadium liked what they saw. Celebrating the 2003 Pan American Games' arrival in the Dominican Republic, 10,000 singers, dancers and artists performed in the opening ceremony as music played and fireworks exploded. Then the nation's greatest current and former baseball pitchers concluded the Games' torch relay.

Boston Red Sox ace Pedro Martinez ran the final leg and handed off to San Francisco Giants great Juan Marichal, who lit a small torch at the edge of the field. Luis Pujols, nephew of the Giants coach of the same name, hit a baseball from that spot into the night sky as the Games' cauldron ignited to wild cheers.

Marichal's Hall of Fame pitching career made him a celebrity in two countries. Famous for his high kick as he reared back to pitch, Marichal won 238 games for the Giants from 1960 to 1973, the most by any pitcher since the team moved to San Francisco. "Juan was the best pitcher I ever saw," said teammate Mike McCormick, an opinion shared by many teammates, opponents and observers.

Marichal earned another distinction after baseball when he became a cabinet member of the Dominican's president. As the nation's sports minister, Marichal helped bring the Pan American Games to Santo Domingo and oversaw the improvement of stadiums and sports facilities from 1996 to 2000. However, accusations of corruption followed the former pitcher and soured his taste for public office.

Marichal grew up in the small village of Laguna Verde in the Dominican Republic, where farm families subsisted on their own rice, corn, bananas, and sweet potatoes. Marichal's father died when he was three.

Today a baseball stadium stands in that village, constructed during Marichal's watch as sports minister. Martinez, Sammy Sosa, and a host of other Dominican stars inspire countless young athletes to pursue sports careers.

Juan Marichal was famous for his high leg kick and pinpoint control.
© S.F. Giants

None of that was true in the 1950s, when no Dominican had ever played in the majors. General Rafael Trujillo's military dictatorship provided Marichal a different introduction to organized ball.

"The dictator's brother was head of the Air Force, and he had a ball team that wasn't supposed to lose," recalled Giants broadcaster Lon Simmons. "Marichal beat them, 1-0. About three days later, there was a knock on his door, and they drafted him into the Air Force to pitch on the team. He was only 16. Then he and another pitcher in a doubleheader each lost, 1-0, and they put them both in the brig."

Released from the military after 14 months, Marichal signed with the Giants at age 19 for $500. To the young man raised in poverty, it was a fortune that supported Marichal through his two years in the Giants farm system. He impressed his Minor League managers.

"He was once brought in with the bases loaded and nobody out," said Simmons. Not yet fluent in English, Marichal asked through the shortstop how the manager wanted him to pitch the hitter. "The manager said, 'Well, low and outside isn't a bad place.' Nine low and outside pitches later, the side was retired and nobody scored."

Marichal one-hit the Philadelphia Phillies in his 1960 Major League debut. Thus began the greatest pitching career in San Francisco Giants history. Marichal pitched six 20-win seasons, and two more with 18 wins, in his 14 seasons with the club. He broke single-season team records for wins (26), complete games (30), shutouts (10), and strikeouts (248).

Players complained about Candlestick Park for decades, but Marichal turned the conditions to his advantage. He quickly realized that the cold, wind, and dust bothered hitters far more than pitchers.

"I never complained," he said during a 2004 visit to San Francisco. "The hitters hated it, but I loved pitching there."

Marichal's high leg kick confounded batters but didn't interfere with his command, said his old battery mate Tom Haller.

"Juan had such great control that you didn't have to worry about the ball being far from where you wanted it," Haller said. "He had a great repertoire." Marichal threw a fastball, screwball, curveball, slider, and changeup, each from three different deliveries: overhand, three-quarters and sidearm.

Marichal no-hit the Houston Colt .45s in 1963. The next month, he followed up with an even more amazing performance at Candlestick. He dueled with Milwaukee Braves pitcher Warren Spahn in a game that reached extra innings in a scoreless tie.

Both starters continued inning after inning, and 25-year-old Marichal refused manager Alvin Dark's offer to bring in a fresher arm. "A 42-year-old man is still pitching," Marichal said. "I can't come out." When Willie Mays hit a home run in the bottom of the sixteenth inning, Marichal registered one of the toughest wins of all time. For his 227-pitch effort, the Giants gave him one extra day of rest before his next start.

"I always felt like Juan was like Picasso, and every game was like a painting," said Simmons, who watched Marichal play for 14 years. "It was amazing the control that he had with that high leg kick. He had a variety of pitches that he threw at different speeds, and good spots."

The one incident that marred his career, and even threatened his induction to the Hall of Fame, occurred during the 1965 pennant race against the Dodgers. Batting against Sandy Koufax, Marichal took a pitch for a strike. Catcher John Roseboro threw the ball back to the mound, nicking Marichal's ear. The two exchanged angry words, and Marichal struck Roseboro's head with his bat.

Blood streamed down Roseboro's face, though his catcher's mask protected him from more serious injury. After Marichal was ejected, an all-out brawl erupted between the teams. Marichal has expressed his regret about the event many times. Yet Roseboro deserves to share the blame, Simmons believes.

"Roseboro was just as guilty as Marichal was," Simmons said. "Roseboro didn't have a bat in his hand, but he threw a ball that nicked Marichal's ear. Marichal had a bat in his hand, and Roseboro came after him. Marichal was backing up when he hit him with the bat.

"Nothing happened to Roseboro. He didn't get a suspension, but Marichal missed about four starts. That cost the Giants the pennant."

Baseball writers vilified Marichal for years, but that didn't change his teammates' opinion of him.

"He's a guy that everybody should have as a friend," said Jim Barr, a Giants pitcher for ten years. "I say that not just because I was a teammate, but because of the way he treated me as a young ballplayer." For instance, the nine-time All Star and his wife would invite the rookie Barr and his wife to eat dinner with them. "Juan and his wife were like that to a lot of young players."

The Giants sold the "Dominican Dandy" to the Red Sox in late 1973. After a season in Boston, Marichal played his last year with, of all teams, the Dodgers.

"They treated me really well," Marichal said. "John Roseboro told the fans that what happened was in the heat of the game and that he wanted the fans to give me a nice welcome."

Marichal retired after the 1975 season, with 243 wins, 142 losses, a 2.89 ERA, 52 shutouts and 244 complete games.

Baseball writers passed on Marichal during his first two years on the Hall of Fame ballot. After Roseboro spoke in favor of his old rival, however, opposition to Marichal's induction evaporated, and Marichal became the Dominican's first Hall of Famer in 1983.

Marichal moved his family back to the Dominican two years after his retirement. He served as the Oakland Athletics' director of Latin American scouting

Marichal became the Dominican Republic's minister of sports.
Photo by Matt Johanson

for 13 years, signing such players as Miguel Tejada.

Then the Dominican's presidential election of 1996 opened a new door. Leonel Fernandez of the Partido de la Liberación Dominicana unseated seven-term President Joaquin Balaguer. The nation's first new leader in more than 30 years asked Marichal to join his cabinet as minister of sports, recreation and physical education. Marichal could hardly refuse.

"They used his popularity and his name to let everybody know that the government, at that time, was interested in sports," said former Giants manager Felipe Alou, another native of the Dominican Republic and former Giants player. "Marichal is a baseball man only, but he had the stature."

As sports minister, Marichal used his $40 million budget to build gymnasiums for basketball and volleyball, a track and field stadium, a boxing arena and other facilities to provide the nation's youth with opportunities to become successful athletes.

But Marichal's term in office was not always pleasant. The government probed allegations in 1999 that officials in his ministry skimmed $6 million through the purchase of sports equipment. In the Dominican, the sports minister oversees cockfighting, a legal activity. But an association of cockfighters also accused Marichal of setting up matches for his personal financial benefit.

Marichal strongly denied the accusations, and claimed his accusers merely wanted to damage his reputation. "I'm a victim of fame," he told the *Listin Diario* newspaper. He refused to respond to the Corruption Prevention Department, though he did appear before a judge for a six-hour interview.

"Anytime you are in a political position like he was, there will be some criticism," said Alou. "But I believe he did a good job, under the circumstances."

President Fernandez lost his re-election bid in 2000, and Marichal left his position that summer as the new administration took office. Though he was never charged, the scandals left their marks on him. As he handed the office keys to successor Cesar Cedeno, he was asked if he would consider holding another public office. "No way," he said. "I would not accept coming back to be the minister of sports or any other post."

Since then, Marichal has operated a baseball academy, one of many such businesses in the Dominican that develops talent for the major leagues. Like many former stars, he sells his signature at sports conventions in the United States, charging $40 to take a photo with fans or $70 to autograph a jersey or bat.

Marichal has also pointed a few prospects towards the Giants, said Peter Magowan, the team's former president.

"He's provided some leads for players in the Dominican Republic," said Magowan. "We actually signed a few."

The Giants honored Marichal with a statue at their ballpark in 2005. He will also be long remembered in the Dominican, where he's the idol of countless boys playing ball on rocky fields with bats made from guava tree branches and crude milk carton gloves.

"Juan Marichal is the symbol of a Dominican big leaguer," said Alou. "He is our Hall of Famer, the only one from the Dominican. But obviously we are going to have many more."

TITO FUENTES

"HOT DOG"

A weary bunch lay on the grass after an all-nighter at the ballpark. The Giants crushed the Dodgers the previous night, 9-3, completing their first four-game sweep of Los Angeles in 29 years. Hundreds of fans carried the celebration onto the field, where they pitched their tents for the team's annual slumber party. A long night of baseball movies and horseplay left a tired crowd for the 7 A.M. wake-up call.

This was a job for Tito Fuentes.

"Hey, ham and bacon, come and get it, come and get it!" shouted a cheerful Fuentes as he toured the field, shaking tents and noisily rousting the campers for their pancake breakfast. The exuberant former Giant is more effective than a stadium full of alarm clocks. "I slept in my hotel and came here fresh in the morning. You think this is going to be hard for me?" he laughed. "No, it's going to be hard for them! When they wake up, the first thing they see is me, and that's no fun."

The smell of fresh coffee reaches the tents. "Oh, the coffee, how did you know?" asked a sleepy camper.

"Of course I know that!" Fuentes roared.

Fuentes is a permanent coffee high, without the coffee. Now a grandfather approaching 70, Fuentes is just as lively as he was during his 13-year Major League career, and nearly as involved in baseball. The former second baseman broadcasts games in Spanish for the Giants and appears at Giants fantasy events and holds baseball clinics for boys clubs and other groups at 24 Willie Mays Plaza when the Giants are on the road.

"He's a ball of fire," said teammate Mike McCormick.

A native of Havana, Cuba, Fuentes learned to play baseball as a youth using a broomstick for a bat and worn-out, tape-covered balls.

"When the cover came off the ball, we bought some tape that we wrapped around the ball to make it last longer," Fuentes said. A neighborhood rule led to

Tito Fuentes fled Cuba to join the Giants in 1962.
© S.F. Giants

some fierce play: "Whoever won the game kept the ball. That was the challenge," he said.

Fuentes played for a national Cuban youth team that won an international championship. Major League scouts pursued him when he was 15, and Fuentes actually signed a contract with the Kansas City Athletics that the commissioner later voided because he was underage.

That cleared the way for the Giants to sign him when he turned 18 in 1962. To become a professional player, Fuentes secretly left Cuba via Mexico, against Cuban restrictions and his father's wishes.

"The revolution took over, and professional was a bad word in Cuba," Fuentes said. "But that's the only thing I always wanted to do."

Segregation forced Fuentes and other black players to live in their team's Florida ballpark in his first Minor League season. "I had to sleep in the training room, and the other guys got two little beds in the manager's room," he said. "We could not go to town or nothing, but we were young and wanted to play."

Fuentes hit .302 and 20 homers for the Giants Triple-A team in Phoenix in 1965, and reached the big club in San Francisco. His enthusiasm showed daily during nine years with the Giants.

"He was so energetic, always so upbeat. He enjoyed baseball so much it would just rub off on you," said Chris Speier, a longtime Giants shortstop and teammate.

For example, Fuentes punctuated each of his at-bats with a ritual in the batter's box. He bounced his bat off home plate, clapped his hands, and caught the bat on the rebound, all without looking. The right hander would stare at the third base coach as he performed his trick. But Fuentes' brassy style of play aggravated competitors throughout the National League.

"There were pitchers who wanted to drill him for it all the time. A few of them actually did," said Speier. "He was a hot dog, but he backed it up."

Even a few Giants objected to Fuentes' style in his rookie year. Before Fuentes mastered English, two players asked pitcher Juan Marichal to express their complaints to him in Spanish.

"They said, 'Hey kid, you cannot play here like that. You're too flashy,'" recalled Fuentes. "I told them, if they don't like the way I play, that's their problem. I'm not going to change."

Speaking Spanish with his teammates actually provided an advantage on the field. When Marichal pitched, Fuentes and Speier could plan pick-offs without alerting the base runners. "They never knew what we were saying, so we got a lot of pick-offs on second base," Fuentes said.

Fuentes enjoyed deceiving opposing base runners and even goading them to hit him sliding into second base: "Five dollars if you can touch me, ten dollars if you knock me down!" They rarely succeeded, and Fuentes' taunts won him few friends on opposing teams.

"If you played against him, you loved to beat him," said Tom Haller, a long-time Giants catcher who played with and against Fuentes. "He could turn the double play pivot as good as anybody, and he was a pesky guy at the plate."

Fuentes' defense endeared him to pitchers like former Giant Jim Barr.

"His hands were so fast when he turned the double play, it was like the ball never hit the glove," said Barr.

Speier, who combined with Fuentes on countless double plays, noticed another quality of his former teammate and future broadcaster.

"He would never shut up," recalled Speier. "Between pitches, he's talking to me. If I won't talk to him, he's talking to the umpire. He's talking to McCovey. He talked to anyone who would talk to him, even during the game."

Fuentes' years with the Giants left an impression on his family. On the day the Giants clinched the National League West title in 1971, Fuentes' son was born, so he named the boy Clinch.

Fuentes' own name reflects his Giants history, too. When he became a United States citizen, he changed his official name to include his old uniform number. "Tito 23 Fuentes" appears on his driver's license and all his official papers. The moniker helps avoid confusion in the family, because 23 gave two of his other children his favorite name: Tito.

After stints with the Padres, Tigers, Athletics, and in Mexico, Fuentes retired as a player in 1978 when he was 33 years old. He finished with a .268 career batting average. Giants fans voted Fuentes as their starting second baseman on the 25th anniversary Dream Team in 1982.

With eight children from two marriages to support and more than ten years before he could draw his baseball pension, Fuentes spent the next decade selling insurance for John Hancock. His notoriety as a ballplayer brought him steady business. "Most of the people used to buy to have me as their agent," Fuentes said. Collaborating with his ex-wife who sold cars, Fuentes sold mostly auto insurance.

Fuentes started calling Giants Spanish radio games in 1982, and expanded his broadcast duties after he left the insurance business.

"In 1996, my big break came," Fuentes said. Fox Sports International hired him to broadcast weekly games that air in Latin America. Eventually, Fox added more games to his schedule, including the playoffs and World Series.

"His style makes you feel like you're on the field making the play yourself," said Gabe Avila, founder of the Hispanic Heritage Baseball Museum. "He's very exciting to hear describing the plays."

In addition to broadcasting, Fuentes enjoys traveling in the off-season. "Every winter, a bunch of us take a trip," he said. "We've gone to India, Vietnam,

Fuentes shares a laugh with former teammates.
Photo by Matt Johanson

China, Tibet, and to Cuba. Life continues. You've got to get the best out of it.
People say I don't look my age because I keep myself busy."

JOHN D'ACQUISTO

"SHARKS IN THE WATER"

In the dugout, John D'Acquisto's cell phone rings to the tune of "Take me out to the Ballgame." The former Giants pitcher-turned-youth coach answers and takes a moment to talk about one of his hottest prospects, a 12-year-old southpaw who already throws 70 miles per hour. Today, though, 12-year-old sluggers roughed him up in a youth league All-Star game.

"Tell him don't even think about quitting at his age, not a left-hander who throws that hard," D'Acquisto says. "Everyone has tough outings, and as he gets older, he'll be better equipped to handle it."

He hangs up, and reflects on the call. "You get at the crossroads where you think about quitting. I want to stay with him. I know he will make me a fine pitcher."

On a muggy summer day on a neighborhood baseball diamond in Chula Vista, California, a few dozen pint-sized ballplayers race around the bases under the watchful eyes of D'Acquisto and his fellow coaches of the MVP Baseball and Softball Academy. A ballplayers' gym with weights and batting cages, the school runs clinics and summer day camps. Each child's family paid $180 for this four-day camp. At each break, the kids flood the dugout for water or a snack.

D'Acquisto's journey from the Giants dugout in Candlestick Park in the 1970s to this one was eventful and turbulent. He pitched for five other teams – the Padres, Expos, Cardinals, Angels and A's – before his final Major League appearance in 1982. After his career ended, he played semi-pro ball and turned to acting, appearing in commercials, television shows, and a Hollywood movie.

But D'Acquisto's main career away from baseball—investment advising and management—led to accusations of securities fraud and forgery, resulting in two federal convictions and six years in prison.

❊❊❊❊❊❊❊

John D'Acquisto struck out 168 batters to set a Giants rookie record in 1974.
© S.F. Giants

The Giants chose D'Acquisto as their first pick in the 1970 draft, when the hard-throwing right hander from San Diego was 19 years old. He played for the Giants' Rookie League affiliate in Great Falls, Montana, attended spring trainings with the big club, and learned from Giants standouts like Juan Marichal.

"Juan taught me a lot about pitching," D'Acquisto said. "He helped me with my control, even though I was still wild."

After throwing a Minor League no-hitter, D'Acquisto broke in to the big club in August 1973, pitching 27 innings in seven games, winning one and losing one with a 3.58 ERA. His fastball was clocked at 100 miles per hour.

That was good enough to make the team the following year in what would be his best season. D'Acquisto struck out 168 batters in 1974 to break a Giants rookie record, winning 12 games and losing 14 in a miserable year for the team: 72 wins, 90 losses, and a fifth-place finish, 30 games behind.

"Those were tough years for the team," D'Acquisto said. "They were in a rebuilding stage. Players were getting older. There was the uncertainty of trade rumors. [Bobby] Bonds was traded. We never had one set manager." In fact, between 1974 and 1979, the Giants employed five different managers: Charlie Fox, Wes Westrum, Bill Rigney, Joe Altobelli and Dave Bristol.

The following year was tough emotionally and physically for D'Acquisto. He was in the midst of a divorce, and he developed a nerve problem in his pitching arm that limited him to ten games, 28 innings and a 10.29 ERA. "The doctors told me that I had a 60-40 chance of coming back. I thought that didn't sound so bad. Then they told me that I was the 40, and not coming back was the 60. 'Do you have a job?' they asked. I was afraid my career was over."

After three months of rehabilitation, however, D'Acquisto returned to pitch in front of empty seats in Candlestick. In 1975 under skipper Wes Westrum, the Giants would improve to 80-81, finishing in third place, but still 27 and a half games out. "We were losing, and there were no fans in the stands," D'Acquisto said. In one game, Giants players counted 436 people in the park, including the vendors.

One highlight for D'Acquisto was receiving an award from Joe DiMaggio on behalf of the Italian American Society as the group's Italian American of the Year for 1975. "I was flabbergasted. That was one of those major highlights that I'll never forget."

D'Acquisto recalls a more intense Giants-Dodgers rivalry in that era.

"On the [clubhouse] wall was a sign that read, 'You will hate Dodger blue,'" he said. "We were out for blood. Now it's more from the front offices, trying to build that rivalry for promotion, but the players hated each other then. We called them crybabies, because every time we beat them, they cried about it. Every time they beat us, we didn't cry, we got mad."

D'Acquisto roomed with fellow pitcher John "The Count" Montefusco on the road, and tried to keep the flamboyant right-hander from overly provoking his opponents.

The Giants in 1976 traded D'Acquisto with Mike Caldwell and Dave Rader to the St. Louis Cardinals for Willie Crawford, John Curtis and Vic Harris. D'Acquisto's final Giants numbers: 18 wins, 27 losses, and a 4.68 ERA.

"John was a guy everybody hated to give up on," recalled Giants broadcaster Lon Simmons. "He had such a great arm, but he could never be consistent. He'd have some control in one game, but in the next one he was liable to hit the guy in the on-deck circle."

None of D'Acquisto's six seasons that followed matched his success in 1974, but his career lasted 10 years, more than enough for a Major League pension. He finished 34-51 overall.

In one memorable game as a Padre, D'Acquisto faced not just his old team, the Giants, but his old roommate, Montefusco. The two dueled for seven scoreless innings, when D'Acquisto came up to bat against the Count.

"He even told me what was coming, sliders," D'Acquisto said with a laugh. "Then he struck me out, the son of a bitch. So when he came up to hit, I struck him out." The Padres scored off Montefusco in the eighth, and went on to win, 4-0, behind D'Acquisto's complete game.

Late in 1982, D'Acquisto played with the Oakland A's under Billy Martin, and came in to face the Kansas City Royals. A good streak of outings ended as he surrendered four runs. It would be his last Major League game. Despite a good spring the following year, the A's passed on him.

In the 1980s, D'Acquisto attempted several comebacks and continued to play semi-pro ball. He appeared in commercials for Miller beer and a supermarket chain, and scored a part in the *Kate and Allie* television series. D'Acquisto played a Kansas City Royals pitcher in the 1991 film, *Talent for the Game*. He and his second wife, Lucia, had a baby boy, John.

Like many players of his era, D'Acquisto carried another job during the off-season. He worked for Bank of America as he played ball in the 1970s, which later led him to try his hand at investment counseling. For a time, he appeared successful. D'Acquisto claims he was close to leading an investment group to buy the San Diego Padres. But a series of events in the 1990s would make him regret he ever entered the world of high finance.

❊ ❊ ❊ ❊ ❊ ❊

On July 13, 1995, the Securities Exchange Commission (SEC) sued D'Acquisto, his partner Thomas Goodman, D'Acquisto's company, the D'Acquisto Financial Group and Doubleday Trust, of which D'Acquisto was a trustee. A civil suit, it would be the first of many legal proceedings against D'Acquisto during the next four years.

The SEC accused D'Acquisto and Goodman in federal court of "engaging in fraudulent schemes involving the offer and sale of securities in a prime bank investment program and an asset enhancement program."

Specifically, "the defendants told one investor that its $200,000 investment would be worth $1,833,565.64 in a week's time by piggybacking the investment to a $500,000,000 'prime bank' transaction," the SEC alleged. "The defendants told a second investor that it would receive returns of 2% to 7.5% per week, and the defendants told a third investor that it would receive returns of at least 80% per month."

In judgment, Judge Marilyn Huff held that "the Defendants committed securities fraud when they obtained approximately $6.5 million from two investors by offering and selling securities in their investment scheme... [The] defendants falsely represented to investors that they were sophisticated money managers, that the investors' funds were secure, the investment was low risk, and that the investment principal and earnings would be returned to investors on a timely basis."

Huff wrote that "the defendants repeatedly violated the law, showed disregard for the law, and represent a risk to the public." The court permanently barred D'Acquisto and Goodman from working as investment advisers and eventually ordered them to repay $7.42 million in "ill-gotten gains" and interest.

D'Acquisto had teamed up with his old Giants roommate Montefusco in the horse racing business around this time. The Count recalled the securities scandal.

"I didn't understand what John was doing," Montefusco said. "Apparently he was milking people for their money and using it for his own personal business. We had fun, though."

D'Acquisto recalls the event differently. "I got set up," he said. "Did I intend to do any of it? No. Did I actually do any of it? No. I was not even connected with the people that actually committed the crime." D'Acquisto alleges that his former partners and even clients conspired to take the money and flee, leaving him to answer questions and face prosecution.

Marianne Wisner, staff attorney of the SEC who handled the case against D'Acquisto, remains satisfied with the outcome. "The court, looking at documentary evidence the SEC submitted, determined that D'Acquisto committed securities fraud," she said.

D'Acquisto declared bankruptcy, but the case didn't end there. Eventually, a criminal trial would follow, but not before D'Acquisto faced another federal charge in an entirely different case.

Police arrested D'Acquisto at his San Diego home in December 1995 for allegedly attempting to pass off a forged $200 million certificate of deposit to Prudential Services, Inc.

D'Acquisto said a client of his business produced the phony certificate, which D'Acquisto handed over to Prudential with instructions to "authenticate before processing."

Yet the feds prosecuted D'Acquisto for forgery, convicting him and sentencing him to 63 months in prison. On Dec. 13, 1996, D'Acquisto began his sentence at Metropolitan Correctional Center, a federal prison in San Diego.

The hardest time, D'Acquisto said, was the first 17 months. On open floors, prisoners shared common rooms with bunk beds. "Animal house," D'Acquisto said. "There were guys killing themselves, hanging themselves from the rafters or cutting their throats... There were fights every day, and not just fights, riots. I'd walk by and let them have at it."

For exercise, prisoners used stationary bicycles or weight machines. The guards sometimes allowed them onto the fenced roof where, in waist- and ankle-chains, they walked around in circles.

"The food was God-awful bad," he said. "It was rotten at some points. You could see the mold in it. They treated us like animals. It was the worst conditions I've ever seen."

While incarcerated, D'Acquisto appealed his ban from working as an investment adviser. His insistence of his innocence would not endear him to the SEC. In his statement filed on April 25, 1997, D'Acquisto wrote that the allegations against him were "false and erroneous," that he did not convert funds of the alleged victims, and that his accusers were in fact the "crooks" who defrauded him.

The SEC noted that D'Acquisto's judge found his actions "particularly egregious because they involved the theft of millions of dollars from investors," and that the fraud occurred over several years and resulted "from a pattern of coordinated acts."

Nor did D'Acquisto's testimony impress the SEC. Because of his alleged offenses and his "failure to accept responsibility for his actions," the SEC concluded that "it is in the public interest to revoke his registration as an investment adviser." When D'Acquisto completed his sentence, he would have to find a different line of work.

❀ ❀ ❀ ❀ ❀ ❀ ❀

Lucia D'Acquisto divorced John in 1999, as he faced criminal charges stemming from the investment scam first addressed in civil court by the SEC in 1995. A grand jury indicted him on 38 counts related to the fraud, and D'Acquisto again appeared in federal court.

"They froze my accounts, so I couldn't even get an attorney. I had to get a public defender," said D'Acquisto.

Though he maintained his innocence, D'Acquisto pled guilty to a single count of fraud. In exchange for his plea, the court granted him a sentence largely concurrent with the remainder of his time on the forgery conviction. In other words, the second case would result in less than a year of additional time.

"A lot of fishy things went on, and I paid the price for it," D'Acquisto said. "My parents suffered. I lost my nephew during that period, he died of leukemia. Generally they let you go to services, but they didn't let me go. I had a lot of trauma, a lot of heartache. I lost my family. I lost my son. They hurt a seven-year-old boy and a woman who's now a single parent trying to make ends meet. That part I didn't like."

Though D'Acquisto accused authorities of wrongfully targeting him, the federal prosecutor who tried D'Acquisto's criminal case believes the outcome was fair. "The government was satisfied with the sentence that was imposed by the court," said William Hayes, who later became chief of the criminal division at the U.S. Attorney's Office in San Diego. "I wouldn't at this juncture attempt to debate Mr. D'Acquisto, but the record speaks for itself."

D'Acquisto was eventually transferred to federal minimum security camp in California's Mohave Desert. He would later go to a similar camp in Florence, Colorado. The camps have no bars or fences, and the inmates work outside of the camps in various capacities. In D'Acquisto's case, this meant assisting the San Bernardino County fire department, among other things.

"They treated you more like a human being. The food was much better," he said.

D'Acquisto worked in the day and would return to the prison at night to sleep.

"I became a full-fledged state of California firefighter, and EMT (emergency medical technician)," he said. "I got to save lives, pull people out of car wrecks, and do good things. It actually worked out pretty good for me."

In 2002, D'Acquisto left prison to start rebuilding his life in the San Diego area. "I worked construction and busted my ass," he said. A friend at a country club employed him for a time in sales and marketing.

But it wouldn't be long before the right hander, then 50 years old, returned to the game. The Giants' dedication of the team's new Willie McCovey statue and history walk reunited him with his teammates in the spring of 2003. He started coaching pitchers at East Lake High School in Chula Vista, and then connected with the MVP Baseball and Softball Academy.

"I get more gratification from showing these kids the fastball, curve and change than you can ask for," he said. "To give back what I learned as a Major League pitcher makes me as proud as you can be."

❊ ❊ ❊ ❊ ❊ ❊ ❊

Back in the dugout, the children crowd in to fetch their lunches after a morning of drills. Some are surprised to find ants in their brown bags, feasting on their sandwiches. As they pick the ants out, D'Acquisto tries to surmise the lesson he learned from his legal experiences.

D'Acquisto eyes his charges at a youth baseball camp.
Photo by Matt Johanson

"My message is to be very careful what you do. Don't get involved in stupid things that are not going to go to the betterment of your life," D'Acquisto says. "I just trusted too many people, and got in with the wrong people. There are a lot of sharks in the water when you're dealing with money. I ran into a couple of them, and ended up taking a fall. It was a lesson to learn, a lesson I'll never forget, but I've come through it OK. And now I'm doing things low-key, working with kids, and doing all the things that I need to do to be a good coach and a good person for these kids."

D'Acquisto's friendship with Montefusco has ended, D'Acquisto said, because Montefusco betrayed him and testified against him before a grand jury. "He ruined my life," D'Acquisto said of his former best friend.

Though Montefusco describes the breakup differently, he agrees that the relationship is over. "I like John and I wish him well," said Montefusco, who became a pitching coach for the Somerset Patriots of the Atlantic League. "But I think I'll stay away from him."

Jay Sundahl, owner of the MVP Academy, says D'Acquisto was a natural fit because of his history as a major leaguer in San Diego and his rapport with the kids.

"I used to watch John pitch as a kid," Sundahl said. "He was one of the few players to throw more than 100 miles per hour. The pop on the glove echoed throughout the stadium. Parents here grew up watching him pitch, so he has some ties that way.

"The kids gravitate to him. He has a great relationship with them," Sundahl adds. "He teaches pitching and throwing mechanics, and his lessons always cover the mental aspects: how to pitch under pressure and when the team behind you makes errors."

D'Acquisto's prosecution and incarceration for financial crimes are "absolutely a non-issue," Sundahl says.

"I was around baseball and I never even knew about it. I think it's more the financial world that would care about that than sports-minded people," Sundahl says. "I've never had a customer, parent or client ever ask about it. We're all about integrity and class. If it was an issue, we wouldn't have him participating. But he adds value to our program."

D'Acquisto hopes to one day return to baseball's big stage in some capacity.

"I follow Major League Baseball because I'm trying to get back in as a coach. I'd like to go back to the Giants organization, because I know so many people there. It would be a very home-like atmosphere for me," he says.

D'Acquisto feels he has something to offer today's Major League pitchers. "I see guys getting ahead 0-2, and throwing the ball down the middle of the plate. You can't do that. When you're ahead, you can waste a pitch. I've never in my whole life seen so many pitchers throwing the ball down the middle. My ball was never straight. It was always moving."

This kids' park seems far away from the majors, though no farther than the leap between federal prison and Chula Vista. D'Acquisto is back in baseball, but is he through with financial counseling?

Most of the kids have gone to the bleachers to eat lunch. The last boy, on his way out of the dugout, picks up some loose change from the cement floor.

"I found 75 cents!" he exclaims.

"Good. Keep it," D'Acquisto replies. "Finders keepers."

JOHN MONTEFUSCO

"I'VE GOT A DREAM AGAIN"

For the first time in 23 years, a beaming John Montefusco took the field in a Giants jersey. As the Giants honored their 1978 team on its twenty-fifth anniversary, "the Count" delighted fans by signing autographs and bragging about the division standings in his remarks.

"I see the Dodgers are where they belong, behind us!" he gloated to a cheering crowd. "Who wants a ball?"

Montefusco clearly enjoyed his brief return to the big stage, perhaps because his time away from the majors has been anything but glamorous. Prior to landing a job as a Minor League pitching coach, Montefusco spent two years in jail before a jury acquitted him of threatening and sexually assaulting his ex-wife. "It was absolute hell," he said. "I really don't know how I got through it."

❊❊❊❊❊❊❊

Montefusco broke in with the Giants in 1974 when he was 24 years old. A hard-throwing right-handed pitcher, the Count quickly became known for three things: his dazzling highlights, his nickname, and his mouth.

"If you want to know how good he was, just ask him and he'll tell you," former Giants broadcaster Joe Angel said.

For instance, as a rookie, Montefusco brashly predicted that he would shut out the Reds and strike out future Hall of Famer Johnny Bench four times. Bench hit a three-run homer as the Reds scored seven runs off Montefusco, who was pulled with one out in the second inning.

"His mouth got him in a lot of trouble," said teammate John D'Acquisto. "I'd say, 'Count, you can't be doing that. These guys are All-Stars. They can hit.' He was very good at waking sleeping dogs."

John Montefusco pitched a no-hitter in 1976.
© S.F. Giants

A few years back, when he was in his mid-fifties, Montefusco claimed he's a changed man.

"If I had it to do over again, I wouldn't be as outspoken as I was," he said. "I was a young kid, and my mouth worked faster than my mind did. I said some really stupid things that I shouldn't have said. It was just because I was naive and immature. I still haven't grown up, but I do watch what I say now.

"I'd like to take back my prediction about Johnny Bench," Montefusco said. "But a lot of my predictions did come true."

If the Count didn't already have a nickname (based on the Alexandre Dumas novel, *The Count of Monte Cristo*), he might well have won the moniker, "the Mouth of San Francisco." Montefusco even claimed part of the credit when Bob Lurie bought the team in 1976, averting a team move to Toronto. "Bob Lurie and I are the reasons the Giants stayed in San Francisco," he proclaimed.

Yet Montefusco's play backed up his talk. Montefusco crowed that he would shut out the Dodgers, for instance, and then beat them, 1-0. He announced that he would throw a no-hitter, which he achieved in 1976.

The Count struck out 215 batters in 1975 to set a Giants rookie record. Behind a 15-9 record, he won Rookie of the Year honors. He finished the next season 16-14, with a 2.85 ERA, 172 strikeouts, six shutouts, and 11 complete games, including his no-hitter against the Braves.

Early in Montefusco's Giants career, he met a young airline stewardess who would soon become Dory Montefusco. They had two daughters together, and their marriage would last 19 years. The idea that accusations of rape and assault would one day destroy the relationship seemed unimaginable to the Montefuscos in 1976, when the Count pitched two shutout innings in the All-Star Game.

❋ ❋ ❋ ❋ ❋ ❋ ❋

During the next season, a series of injuries coincided with a decline in Montefusco's performance on the field.

"In May of '77, I broke my ankle against the Reds," Montefusco said. "I tried to beat out a play at first. I had just signed a five-year contract, and I went on the disabled list for the first time. I felt guilty about collecting money on the DL, and it killed me. The next thing I know, everything else went, and I was never the same pitcher again."

A fight with his manager Dave Bristol soured the Count's Giants tenure further. During an angry post-game exchange in Bristol's office, Montefusco suffered a black eye and placed Bristol into a headlock.

"When I got in the fight with Bristol, I said some things I shouldn't have, and I wish I could take that back," Montefusco said.

The Giants traded Montefusco to the Braves in 1980. The Count's career lasted six more seasons as he learned to pitch effectively with less power. His injuries forced the change; a hip problem became acute and eventually required replacement surgery.

"If you can strike people out when you're in trouble, the game is easy," Montefusco said. "But if you can't get that strikeout, then the game is tough. That's what happened to me, so I had to learn to pitch."

Though he once threw only fastballs and sliders, Montefusco learned to "change speeds, spot the ball, sink the ball, and come up with a splitter and a change up."

Montefusco's best year away from the Giants came in 1983 with the Padres and Yankees when Montefusco won 14 games against four losses. He played his last game in a Yankees uniform in 1986.

"We were playing against Minnesota. I pitched a couple of innings and gave up a few homers," he said. Doctors told Montefusco that his hip replacement surgery during the previous off-season would end his career. Though the Count made the Yankees roster as a reliever, the doctors were soon proved right. "My hip just couldn't take it. I had to retire," Montefusco said. He was 36.

❀ ❀ ❀ ❀ ❀ ❀

Then the Count landed a job as executive host of a Donald Trump casino in Atlantic City. The job involved identifying high-rolling gamblers, or "whales," and giving them whatever it took to keep them in the casino.

But Montefusco found the low-rolling "fleas" to be irritating. "Fleas want everything in the world from you, and you can't give it to them," he said. "They hound you all day long. I just got sick of it." A year and a half later, Montefusco gave it up.

The Count's boyhood love of horses led to his next venture. As a teenager in Keansburg, New Jersey, Montefusco walked thoroughbreds at Monmouth Park for a dollar each. Even while playing for the Giants, Montefusco worked as a publicity assistant at Bay Meadows Racetrack in San Mateo. So at 41, Montefusco began a career as a harness racer, winning his first race on a horse named Angel Beside Me on Oct. 20, 1991. He received a winner's share of $27.

"After I won my first race, I was hooked," he said, and not on the money. Rather, the Count relished the return to competition after his retirement from baseball had come much too soon. "It was fun, it was dangerous, it was an absolute thrill," he said. During the next few years, Montefusco competed in more than 100 races, including one in his old Giants jersey.

Montefusco also rejoined his old Giants teammate D'Acquisto in thoroughbred racing. D'Acquisto supplied the money, and the Count picked horses to buy and race. Montefusco worked briefly as a pitching instructor at a Yankees minicamp.

But Montefusco also struggled with an addiction to painkillers he started taking after his hip replacement surgery. D'Acquisto soon came under fire for investment fraud, and their friendship and business relationship ended bitterly. The Montefuscos had trouble paying their bills, and lost their lavish New Jersey home in 1996.

When police were summoned to the Montefuscos' new residence in March 1997, the Count's life changed forever.

❈ ❈ ❈ ❈ ❈ ❈

Both Montefuscos agreed that they argued that morning. But Dory said that John attacked her, a charge that John vehemently denies. The police arrested John for assault, and the couple separated later that year. They would eventually divorce, but the dispute didn't end there.

Dory accused John of threatening her with a knife, multiple assaults and rape in October 1997. John said they had consensual sex, that he never struck her, and that Dory was the one who brandished the knife on a separate occasion. Later John allegedly broke a restraining order by confronting his wife at her home about the charges, to ask her "why she did it, why she ruined my life," as he later told a jury. Police arrested him again and bail was set at $1 million.

"I sat in jail because I wouldn't make a deal with the prosecutors' office," Montefusco said. He turned down the prosecution's offer to plead guilty to aggravated assault. "I wouldn't plead to aggravated assault because I wouldn't say that I hit her. If I accepted that deal, people would say, 'He admitted to hitting her, he probably did everything else.'"

A busy court calendar and several changes of attorneys delayed Montefusco's trial for two years. Unable to raise the $1 million bail, Montefusco spent those years in a two-man cell, eight feet wide by ten feet long, at the maximum-security Monmouth County (New Jersey) Jail.

The time felt like an eternity to the man who was once a flamboyant baseball star. Weeks passed before he could bring himself to eat much of the jail's food. Montefusco was once dragged into a fight, he said, landing him in the J-pod solitary lock-up for three days. Yet solitary confinement was a brief relief from the pressure of living among the other inmates. "Every hour was like a day, every day like a week, and so on and so on," he said. "You had to keep your eyes open and your mouth shut. I got beat up a couple of times. It wasn't nice."

Years after his release, the experience still haunts him. "I still have nightmares about it," Montefusco said. "It has not gone away from me, and I don't think it will ever go away from me. Those two years I never thought I'd get through. There were times when they gave out razors, and I was thinking about breaking one open, taking the blade out, and doing something harmful to myself to just end it."

But he didn't, "because of my kids and because I wanted to prove that I was innocent. I did not want to give her the satisfaction. I put up with the time."

Montefusco could not fathom why Dory accused him of such crimes at the time of his arrest, but he later found an explanation. While Montefusco awaited trial in jail, Dory's father became ill and died. His will stipulated that Dory would receive only interest on the multi-million dollar trust, if she was still married to John at the time of her father's death. However, she could terminate the trust and get all the money up front if she and John had divorced. To John, this was "the piece of the puzzle that made everything fit."

"When I saw the will, I couldn't believe it," he said. "We had gone through my money. Her dad was a penny pincher. He was probably afraid that if I got hold of his money, the money he wanted for his daughter would be gone. But unbeknownst to him, she was the one who spent all the money."

During the trial in November 1999, Dory Montefusco testified that she feared for her life the night John allegedly attacked her. She told the jurors that at the time, she thought, "This must be what it is like to die."

John testified that he did not and could not harm his ex-wife or anyone. "I couldn't even spank my children when they were little," he said. In addition, he told the court what he had learned about his father-in-law's will.

The jurors found John more convincing. After a two-week trial, they deliberated three hours before acquitting him of all original 18 counts, including sexual assault. They convicted him of misdemeanor assault and trespassing.

"For him to get away with it is astonishing," Dory said after the trial. "I think he's a sociopath who is a pathological liar. I think he's probably horrified by the things he did and doesn't want to believe he did them."

At sentencing, prosecutor Anita White told the judge, "No one should have suffered the treatment that [Dory Montefusco] received from the defendant, John Montefusco... She's in fear for her life." The judge sentenced John to three years' probation.

John, however, says that he was the victim in the case, and that his "absolutely evil" ex-wife belongs in jail for "lying to the grand jury and lying on the witness stand."

"My vindication was that I turned around and sued her for all the false things she had me put in jail for," he said. The settlement was "very good for me," he said, though he added, "Nothing will ever make up for what I went through. If you're innocent, jail is the worst thing that can happen to you."

❈ ❈ ❈ ❈ ❈ ❈

The Count returned to baseball in 2000. The Somerset (New Jersey) Patriots of the Atlantic League needed a pitching coach, and their manager Sparky Lyle sold the team on Montefusco. "Sparky gave me a chance and fought to get me the job," Montefusco said. "I interviewed with the general manager and also with the owner. They saw I was a fair person and let me have the job."

Montefusco revives the 1970s Giants' look during a visit to Pacific Bell Park.
Photo by Matt Johanson

The Patriots draw between 5,000 and 7,000 fans most nights. The team drives thousands of miles per season. Players and coaches carry their own luggage. It's not the majors, but the Count considered himself a lucky man.

"It's better than I thought it would be," he said. "Everybody wants to be with a Major League organization, but with Sparky around, with the front office that we have, and especially the owner Steven Kalafer, it feels like a Major League organization. He's a great owner. He'll do anything for us and get us anything we need."

Montefusco's advice to young pitchers is simple: get ahead with fastballs, and finish them off with breaking balls. Don't give the hitters too much credit. Throw strikes and get them out. But as a coach, the Count has gained a new perspective on young, cocky athletes.

"What goes around comes around, and I'm getting it now from the players," Montefusco said. "It's only fair to reap what you sow, and now it's come back to me. I have some players I cannot put up with, but as a coach, you have to bite your tongue and keep your mouth shut.

"They run off at the mouth. They think they know everything, just like I thought I knew everything," said the Count. "They think that Sparky and I never played before. We're trying to help these kids, and they don't want to hear a word from us. The only time they want to come to us is when they're not winning, when the hitters are in a slump or when the pitchers can't get anybody out. That's the only time, when they're afraid they may get released. I'm talking about the ones that are tough to handle.

"Granted, there are a bunch of good kids out there who do listen," Montefusco said. "I really like working with the kids. I love watching them get picked up and move on."

In 2003, the Patriots made the playoffs on the last day of the season, and won the Atlantic League championship, largely on the strength of their pitching. "It just seemed like the pitching came around," Montefusco said. "It took me and Sparky half the season to understand the pitchers that we had. Then we did the right things with them and made the right moves."

On and off the field, Montefusco and his daughters made up for lost time. Gina and Allie Montefusco lived close enough to attend many Patriots home games, much to the delight of their father. "It's nice to have them coming to the games," he said. "I just don't want them going out with a ballplayer."

The Count still dreams of a return to the majors as a pitching coach.

"As a kid, my dream was to get to the big leagues as a player," he said. "After I finished playing, I didn't have any more dreams. But I've got a dream again and I'm going to try to achieve it. Hopefully it will be with the Giants."

WILLIE McCOVEY

STRETCHING FOR RECOVERY

Willie McCovey still thrills a crowd. More than 30 years after he last played, the former Giant draws a standing ovation at every ballpark appearance. The Giants' favorite body of water and a successful restaurant bear his name. No Giant was ever more popular than "Stretch," the lanky left-hander who routinely whacked baseballs over Candlestick Park's right field fence.

"I guess I've come a long ways from that young guy in Mobile, Alabama to having a statue here in San Francisco," McCovey said in 2003 when the Giants unveiled his bronze likeness at China Basin Park.

But McCovey's success came at a terrible price. After a 22-year career full of injuries, he began a retirement full of surgeries. McCovey has painfully struggled with back problems and ruined knees that have restricted him to crutches and wheelchairs for years.

"He's gone through a lot," said Lon Simmons, longtime Giants broadcaster and friend of McCovey. "Each time it appears that the doctors have found what to do, something else screws up. I don't know how many surgeries he's had."

McCovey exploded into the Giants lineup as a rookie on July 30, 1959. He hit two singles and two triples against the Phillies' future Hall of Famer Robin Roberts, starting a torrid run that won him Rookie of the Year honors in only 52 games. In a career of highlights, this is among McCovey's favorites. "It's hard to beat my opening day when I went four for four," he said.

McCovey started in left field but played most of his career at first base. At six-feet-four, his uncanny ability to reach the ball while staying on the bag earned him the nickname "Stretch." He led the league in RBIs twice and in home runs three times, winning the 1969 National League MVP award.

"He was a great lowball hitter," said former Giants catcher Tom Haller. "He had more trouble with the ball up, but if you made a mistake, he'd kill you."

Willie McCovey was the National League's Most Valuable Player in 1969.
© S.F. Giants

McCovey usually batted in the cleanup position, protecting teammate Willie Mays.

"When I hit a double, I'd always stop at first to make sure that Mac could hit," joked Mays at McCovey's statue unveiling. "And he could hit. I did that many times, and I got in trouble because of that."

Arthritic knees and bone chips in his hips took a toll as McCovey's play declined in the 1970s. Even McCovey didn't know that those knee problems would later restrict him to crutches and walkers before the age of 60.

"I played my whole career injured, my whole career," McCovey said. "It started probably in my second year in the minor leagues when I hurt my knee, when I played in the Texas League in Dallas. Ever since then I've had knee problems."

The Giants traded McCovey to San Diego prior to the 1974 season, where he hit .253 over the next two years. His average dropped to .203 in 1976 when the Padres sold him to Oakland. McCovey appeared in just 11 games for the Athletics, who released him at the season's end.

McCovey's career appeared over, but Stretch asked the Giants to give him a tryout in the spring of 1977. "I can still hit homers," he told the management, "and if I wasn't 100 percent sure that I could make this club, I wouldn't be here."

Not only did McCovey make the team at age 39, but he batted .280 with 28 home runs and 86 RBIs in his best season since 1970. On Willie McCovey Day at Candlestick Park that September, he beat Cincinnati with a ninth-inning RBI single. He was an easy winner of the National League's Comeback Player of the Year award.

The end arrived in 1980, when Dave Bristol managed the Giants.

"Dave Bristol did not treat him very well," said former Giants broadcaster Hank Greenwald. "He thought McCovey was holding back Mike Ivie and he wanted him out." Ivie, 27, hit .241 for the Giants in 1980, mostly at first base. McCovey announced his mid-season retirement and played his last game July 10 at Dodger Stadium.

"Bristol didn't even start him in his last game," Greenwald said. "Willie had had enough of him at that time, too. I was on the air when he had his final at-bat, as a pinch hitter. The ovation he received was heartwarming. It was all you could do to choke back the tears."

During 19 seasons with the Giants, McCovey established San Francisco records in games (2,256), home runs (469) and RBIs (1,388). A six-time All-Star, he hit 521 home runs and a league-record 18 grand slams.

Through it all, McCovey impressed his teammates and the baseball establishment with his dedication to the community. He started the March of Dimes Golf Classic in 1978, which raised millions of dollars for the charity that strives to prevent birth defects and infant mortality. He would serve as the chairman of the Northern California March of Dimes for years.

"They don't give awards for a man who takes his time and visits children's hospitals and children's wards in hospitals and spends his time throughout the community," said Peter Ueberroth, former commissioner of baseball, when McCovey entered the Hall of Fame in 1986. "He did it as a selfless gesture all through his career. Not much written about it, and he doesn't want much written about it."

In his induction speech, McCovey thanked many family members, teammates and friends, including the Dudum family of San Francisco. Jeff Dudum would one day open McCovey's Restaurant in Walnut Creek.

As a Hall of Famer and member of the 500 home run club, Stretch enjoyed high demand for autographs and appearances at card shows. But McCovey's involvement in a 1989 convention in Atlantic City led to federal tax-evasion charges.

McCovey pleaded guilty in 1995 to not reporting $33,000 in cash he received from the show, and also admitted he failed to report $70,000 from other appearances.

"I've always tried to do the right things," McCovey told Judge Edward Korman. "I have never willingly tried to cheat the government, and it's one of those things that was overlooked at the time and I do accept responsibility for it."

The show's promoter was sentenced to 14 months in prison. But community members rallied around McCovey, including San Francisco's newly-seated Mayor Willie Brown. "Willie McCovey has been, above all else, loyal to the good things that matter in life: loyal to a set of values that put the right priority on giving to others, loyal to fans and the hometown that cheered him on, and loyal to the children and the needy who need a champion to be there for them," Brown wrote the court.

Requesting leniency, McCovey's attorney revealed that he would soon undergo full reconstruction of both knees and suffered from a debilitating spinal problem. The judge sentenced him to two years probation and a $5,000 fine.

McCovey said the experience was "more positive than negative" in an interview with the *San Francisco Examiner*. "So many people, from the mayor on down, rallied behind me. I don't think it was as big of an issue as it was in the newspapers," he said.

Each September, the Giants choose an inspirational player to receive the Willie Mac Award, honoring the Giant who "best exemplifies the spirit and leadership consistently shown by McCovey throughout his career." McCovey usually presents the award at an on-field ceremony, though his knee problems have caused him to miss a few years.

The players often vote for a teammate who overcame adversity during the year. First baseman J.T. Snow won the award in 1997, the year he was hit in the face by a Randy Johnson fastball, and again in 2004.

"It's neat because it's voted on by your teammates, and the name Willie McCovey speaks for itself," Snow said. "I didn't realize how big it was until I started talking to fans who've followed the Giants for a long time. They told me what a special award it was and about all the previous guys who have won it."

Pitcher Mark Gardner won the award in 2001, when his wife Lori had a second liver transplant in her struggle with cancer. She died two years later.

"Obviously Willie McCovey is somebody that a lot of people look up to in this organization," said Gardner, who became the team's bullpen coach. "It's one of the highest honors I've ever received, if not the highest. Just him being here that night, being able to snap a photo with him, and putting my name underneath his was just awesome."

McCovey joined the Giants front office in 2000. As senior advisor, he's available as a resource for the owners, management and players. "If somebody wants to know something and wants my advice, he comes to me," McCovey said. "Players don't ask questions as much as they used to when I was playing, but there are still a few who ask some advice when they're in a slump or want me to watch them. I'm not the type that's going to step on the hitting coach's toes."

The presence of McCovey, Mays, and other former stars pays important benefits, says former Giants manager Felipe Alou.

"I believe the most important part of the Giants tradition is the great players that this club has," said Alou. "Anybody that comes over here, they know they're not coming to play for a drug store team. I mean, this is the team of Willie Mays, Orlando Cepeda, Willie McCovey, Bobby and Barry Bonds, Gaylord Perry and Juan Marichal. We don't have the monuments in center field like they do in New York, but the guys are still here, the majority of them. Therefore it is a demanding situation.

"I believe that any player who comes here knows he's coming to a place that wins," Alou said. "The fans know a good player when they see one. I believe that's the biggest help for the guys. It elevates their game."

Former Giants President Peter Magowan made a point to include former players like McCovey since his ownership group bought the team in 1992.

"It's a big thing for the players to see him in the clubhouse as much as he's there," said Magowan. "And it also shows them that once their careers are over, the Giants don't forget these people. We've got quite a few former players working in the organization in various capacities."

McCovey's poor mobility has limited his role, Magowan said. He uses a golf cart to get around the ballpark.

"It's not good," Magowan said of McCovey's condition. "He keeps hoping, but after 12 or 13 operations, it's hard not to get discouraged."

Actually, McCovey has had more surgeries than that. "Way more," he said.

"He's had the knees replaced and replaced again," said Simmons. "He's had cadaver ligaments put in. He's just had all sorts of difficulties with them. It's amazing how well he's taken it, how he hasn't become bitter about it. He's really faced up to it beautifully, much better than most people would have."

McCovey attends most Giants home games.
Photo by Matt Johanson

McCovey's Restaurant opened in 2003. Stretch himself helped design the memorabilia layout; signed jerseys, balls, bats, and pictures fill the dining room from floor to ceiling. Co-owner Jeff Dudum wanted the restaurant to incorporate two big parts of McCovey's life: baseball and family. One of ten siblings, McCovey has a daughter and grandchildren.

"It's been a good experience so far," said McCovey, a partner in the business. "I enjoy being there and meeting the people. The concept came from Jeff Dudum. Naturally he had to run everything through me for the final say."

McCovey often visits the restaurant, where he has a private room and has continued his support of charities. Benefits have raised money for Little League and the Special Olympics.

He has everything he wants, except his health.

"I'm doing everything I'd like to do right now, though I'd like to get back on the golf course. That's what I'm looking forward to," he said.

JIM
BARR

TALENT RUNS IN THE FAMILY

The Barr girls learned from a pro at a young age. They could hardly avoid it, because their father, Giants pitcher Jim Barr, put them to work as battery mates when they were still in elementary school.

"During the off-season, he would make me be his catcher," recalled Emmy Barr, the older daughter, who was nine when her father retired from the majors in 1983. "He would take me out in front of our house and give me a catching mitt. He'd have to bribe me because I didn't like doing it. But he was pretty good at throwing right to the glove. As long as he did that, I would catch the ball."

Betsy Barr was only two when her father retired. But she was drafted to catch too, when she was old enough, as Jim continued to pitch in a summer league and work out each evening.

"He wasn't throwing as hard as he could, but he still had action on his ball," Betsy said. "And every once in a while, he'd call to my mom, 'Susie, come out and pretend like you're a batter.'"

Two decades later, the Barr daughters became professional athletes themselves, though not as catchers or in baseball. After their successful collegiate soccer careers, both joined the Women's United Soccer Association, Emmy with the Washington Freedom and Betsy with the San Jose CyberRays.

Their father, meanwhile, stayed close to the game he knows best as pitching coach of the Sacramento State University baseball team. A 12-year Major League veteran, Barr considered coaching professionals, but decided instead to join the Hornets, in part to remain close to his Granite Bay home and family.

"It's fun. I enjoy it," said Barr, a Giant for ten years. "I thought about coaching at the Minor League level, but that would have meant being away from home seven months out of the year. In the long run, this was good for me. I had two

Jim Barr won 90 games in 10 seasons as a Giants starter and reliever.
© S.F. Giants

daughters in college playing soccer. This gave me the opportunity to watch them play."

✿✿✿✿✿✿✿

Barr won 90 games as a Giant and 101 games in his career, starting on the Giants' National League West championship team of 1971.

The Giants would finish with winning records in just two of the next seven seasons, but Barr set a record in 1972 by retiring 41 straight batters over two games against the Pirates and Cardinals.

"I was the kind of pitcher that didn't strike out very many guys, but I put the ball in play," Barr said. "Pittsburgh and St. Louis were free-swinging clubs at that time. I'd throw low and away and they'd hit the ball on the ground."

Barr was astonished when the radio broadcasters informed him he'd broken a Major League record. "I said, 'Wow, you got to be kidding.' I had no clue what they were talking about," he said.

Barr's most productive season came in 1976, when he won 15 games against 12 losses, pitching a career-high 252 innings with a 2.89 ERA.

"It was so much fun playing behind Jim," said Chris Speier, longtime Giants shortstop. "He worked fast and he threw strikes. He had such great control that he made it easy to anticipate. And he was such a competitor. He didn't have that fantastic stuff that blew people away, but he had a real bulldog mentality."

Broadcaster Hank Greenwald agreed. "He had that killer instinct that it takes, the kind that you wish some pitchers had today," said Greenwald, who recalled a heated argument between the pitcher and manager Frank Robinson that once erupted when the skipper pulled Barr from a game. Furious at Robinson's decision, Barr flipped the ball to his manager instead of handing it over before he stormed off the field. It was very unlike "Gentleman Jim," but at the time, Greenwald said, "He was in another world."

Following a difficult 1980 season with the Angels, Barr spent all of 1981 in the minor leagues. He contacted the Giants prior to the 1982 season, and the team invited him to try out during Spring Training.

Barr made the team and ranks the Opening Day standing ovation he received at Candlestick Park among his favorite career memories.

"That probably stands out in my mind as much if not more than some of the games that I pitched," said Barr. "To play for a team, leave, come back and have people still like you means a lot. Players have big egos. If we got the money to play in an empty stadium, it wouldn't be the same."

Before his retirement, Barr and a neighbor started a construction business in the Sacramento area. Later, Barr owned and operated a Burger King restaurant for 12 years.

"I enjoyed it, though I wouldn't say it was fun," Barr said. "If you like the fast food business, you like it. If you don't, it will beat you down. I had a lot of longtime employees. I wasn't a guy who would fire somebody for making a mistake.

"The food isn't that bad," he added. "A lot of people eat it, though there are probably healthier choices."

Barr began coaching Sacramento State pitchers in 1995, at the invitation of head coach John Smith. A NCAA Division I team, the Hornets have 11 scholarships and a traveling roster of 25 players. The program is competitive and has sent players to the pros, though college-level baseball is as far as most of them expect to get, Barr said.

"When I first got there, I thought a lot of them were looking to go on and play pro ball," Barr said. "Actually that's not the case. Maybe only three or four of them per year really have the ability to go on. The majority of them just want to play college ball, get their degree and get on with life."

The Giants' difficult years in the mid-1970s actually prepared Barr to better coach his players, he said.

"In '73, '74 and '75, we didn't have a very good defense," Barr said. "In fact, one year we led all the major leagues as the worst defensively, and the next year we were second-worst. We didn't have a very good offense either.

"When I'm coaching now, I use some of the things I experienced back when I was playing. I can tell them, 'I know what you're going through, when you have to throw a shutout to tie.'"

During and after Jim's Major League career, the Barr girls learned a variety of sports, encouraged and coached by both of their parents. Baseball and softball were among their pursuits, but soccer proved the strongest attraction. Betsy recalled an early experience playing goalie against her older sister.

"My mom always coached my sister's team, and every time they had practice, I would go with them," said Betsy. "They'd stick me in the goal and shoot on me. They were only 10 or 11 years old, so their shots weren't too hard." Betsy was only four at the time.

Emmy, a defender, played for Santa Clara University until she graduated in 1997. There was no women's professional soccer league then, but she continued training and playing until the WUSA launched in 2001.

"I give Emmy a lot of credit," said her father. "Out of college, she played semi-pro for three years. She stayed in shape, good enough to get drafted in the top five rounds."

Betsy, a midfielder, helped the University of Portland win the NCAA championship in 2002. The CyberRays drafted her prior to the 2003 season.

Their parents have enjoyed watching them over the years.

"It's a good sport," Barr said. "A lot of people think there's just not enough action in it. I disagree because I've been around the game so much that I know how to watch the game. It's different than baseball, and it's not like football. There's continual action."

The daughters faced each other as opponents for the first time in 2003, when Emmy's Freedom beat Betsy's CyberRays twice. Betsy may have to wait a while

Barr raised two professional soccer players
and coaches pitchers at Sacramento State university.
Sacramento State University photo

to pay her sister back, though, because the WUSA cancelled its 2004 season under financial constraints.

Both Barrs kept training to resume their professional careers if and when the league restarts play, showing discipline not unlike their father's, as he hurled baseballs against a tarp in the backyard well into his fifties.

"He always made it clear that you have to work when no one's watching," said Emmy. "You work out on your own, so that when game time comes, that's your time to shine."

That's the attitude that made both Barr daughters successful, said their father.

"They're both workaholics, working out all the time," Barr said. "I guess part of me rubbed off on them in a nice way."

Where Have You Gone?

FRANK ROBINSON

AS FRANK AS EVER

When the Montreal Expos botched a pop-up and allowed the Giants to score the tying run, they immediately started arguing with the home plate umpire over the infield fly rule. Skipper Frank Robinson marched onto the field and, instead of taking their side, chewed them out in front of a packed house.

"You don't know the game," he shouted. "Get out of here!"

Twenty years had passed since Robinson managed the Giants, but the 68-year-old flashed his familiar fire during his Expos' 2003 visit to 24 Willie Mays Plaza.

"The players were arguing. He pushed all of them off," recalled former Giants manager Felipe Alou with a laugh. "I understood exactly where he was coming from. He didn't want any silliness out there."

Giants players considered Robinson shrewd but demanding when he led the Giants for three-and-a-half seasons in the early 1980s. He had a similar reputation in his stellar playing career, hitting 586 home runs, mostly with Cincinnati and Baltimore.

Robinson tried to explain his intensity when he entered Cooperstown in 1982 with a story from his Oakland youth. Sliding into second base, he ripped his pants and bloodied his knees. "I didn't think too much about it until I got home and my mother scolded me," he said. "I think that was the stage that set the determination in the way I played the game. And a lot of people say there's nothing wrong with that, that's the way baseball is supposed to be played. You're supposed to slide … But what you don't realize is that field was covered by asphalt."

After a parade of managers failed to produce success in the 1970s, the Giants looked to the Hall of Famer to reverse their fortunes in 1981. Robinson's insight and passion for the game were unquestioned, but many players found his high

Hall of Famer Frank Robinson managed the Giants from 1981 to 1984.
© S.F. Giants

standards and forceful personality intimidating.

"I think Frank Robinson was such a gifted athlete that he found it hard for players not to play like a Frank Robinson," said Dan Gladden, a rookie during the skipper's San Francisco tenure. "But there are very few people who can play at his level."

Under Robinson, the Giants contended until the last weekend in 1982. Though they faltered and finished third, they knocked the Dodgers out of the playoffs in a dramatic victory on the last day of the season. The team slipped in 1983 and plummeted in 1984. The Giants fired him on August 4, with 42 wins and 64 losses.

"We were in Atlanta when he got fired," Gladden said. "And when he started the meeting off, he said, 'Now that I'm being fired, Danny Gladden is probably the happiest guy in here.' Not knowing where he was going with this story, I was a little confused. Then he says, 'Because he missed two signs last night and now he won't have to pay the $200 fine.'"

Robinson landed some tough assignments since then. When he took the Orioles' helm in 1988, Baltimore opened the season with a record 21 straight losses. Robinson and the Orioles rebounded in 1989, finishing second as the skipper won the American League Manager of the Year award. He later worked as baseball's dean of discipline, handing out suspensions and fines for violations like fighting.

Baseball Commissioner Bud Selig suggested eliminating the perennially struggling Expos in 2001. Instead, the Major League Baseball owners collectively bought the team and hired Robinson to manage while they pursued a new home for the franchise.

Robinson led the team to a winning record and a second-place finish in 2002. Starved for support in Montreal, the Expos began playing a portion of their home games in San Juan, Puerto Rico in 2003, traveling more miles than any other team. Ten players spent a total of 751 games on the disabled list. Still, the Expos matched their 83-79 record of the previous year.

After losing star right fielder Vladimir Guerrero and ace pitcher Javier Vazquez to free agency, 2004 was a tougher season. The Expos fell to last place before empty seats in Olympic Stadium. Relations strained between the manager and his players. Before one game, the frustrated skipper posted a blank lineup card in the clubhouse beside a curt note: "Anyone who really wants to play, write your name in the lineup." Only one bench player signed his name.

The fans and the press called for Robinson's head, but observers familiar with the Expos' depleted roster were impressed that he achieved any success with a franchise so close to death. Constantly losing top players made managing in Montreal a frustrating proposition, said Alou, who led the Expos from 1992 to 2001.

"In Montreal, you're not going to let go guys like Guerrero and Vasquez and

Robinson led the Expos to two winning seasons
before the team slipped to last place in 2004.
Photo by Matt Johanson

replace them with better guys," said Alou. "You replace them with Double-A guys that were prospects." When Alou managed the team, he watched as slugger Larry Walker, pitcher Pedro Martinez, and even his All-Star son Moises Alou left for richer teams.

When Robinson entered the Hall of Fame, he gave the public a rare glimpse into his thoughts about himself and how he relates to people. "Maybe I am a little tough on people, maybe I am a little standoffish," he said. "I have tried to change for the better, and to this day some people say that's not too much. But I assure you that it's much better than I used to be."

As he neared 70, Robinson allowed himself a few laughs and light moments in the clubhouse that would once have been totally out of character. His patience and geniality surprised some of his players.

"Maybe he's mellowed out," said Expos outfielder Brad Wilkerson. "As long as we're giving the effort, he can deal with a mistake or two... He's very approachable. He has an open-door policy. And I think that helps the youngsters loosen up a little bit."

Pitcher T.J. Tucker expressed similar sentiments until the skipper cut him short and ordered him to a team meeting. "Would you care to join us?" Robinson yelled across the room. "Stop saying all those good things about me!"

After the Expos moved and became the Washington Nationals, Robinson worked for the commissioner's office and became a Major League Baseball executive vice president.

JACK CLARK

"I'm Not a Dodger"

When he coached the Dodgers, Jack Clark always wore a jacket. He was the only one on the team who never took his off, because it covered his name and his number 22 on the back of his Los Angeles jersey.

"Hey Jack, it's sure hot out here, isn't it?" a fellow coach taunted him one blazing afternoon.

"Yes it is," answered Clark. "But I'm not letting anybody see Jack Clark wear a Dodger uniform."

Clark coached Dodgers hitters for two-and-a-half years, garnering high praise from his players even when Los Angeles floundered offensively. But the longtime Giants slugger was never comfortable in Dodger blue.

"I'm not a Dodger, and I felt really weird wearing that uniform," said Clark. "I didn't like it because I'm loyal that way, but when I called, I was turned down by the Giants and the Cardinals. The only ones that really offered me anything were the Dodgers."

Clark struggled to recover from serious injuries he sustained in a motorcycle accident that nearly claimed his life before the Dodgers fired him in 2003. He also coached and managed Minor League teams, though he wants to return to the majors. "I think I'm the best hitting coach in baseball and not in the big leagues," he said.

❀ ❀ ❀ ❀ ❀ ❀ ❀

Jack "the Ripper" Clark joined the Giants as a 19-year-old rookie in 1975, just two years out of Gladstone High School in the San Gabriel Valley.

"I grew up in Southern California, but I always liked the Giants," Clark said. "They were the only team I wanted to play for. They had the right color uniforms, and their style of play matched my personality. Marichal, Mays,

Jack Clark knocked in a team-record 21 game-winning runs in 1982.
© S.F. Giants

McCovey, and [Bobby] Bonds... The Dodgers didn't have anybody like that."

By 1978, the right fielder was an All-Star, hitting .306 with 25 home runs. The Ripper hit in 26 straight games that season, and registered 21 game-winning RBIs in 1982, both San Francisco records. He led the Giants in home runs and RBIs four different years.

"The Ripper hit the ball harder than anybody I've seen," said teammate Dan Gladden. "Infielders would back off when he took batting practice."

But Clark often seemed unhappy on a team that rarely contended and never reached the playoffs during his ten-year stay. Honest to a fault, Clark has never been afraid to tell it like he sees it, and he didn't hesitate to criticize Giants management for its failure to produce a stronger team. "This organization is a loser," he declared in 1982.

"He was a guy who was somewhat misunderstood," said former Giants broadcaster Hank Greenwald. "People thought of him as petulant at times, and I think it was largely because he was not as articulate at that stage in his life as he is today. He was frustrated because he felt the Giants would never get any better. The Giants at that time didn't know how to put together a winning team. That frustration came out, and people mistook him for being a bad egg."

Today Clark believes the Giants' lack of veterans, including those who attracted him to the team in the first place, was a main weakness during his Candlestick Park days.

"We weren't handed a very good formula or a very good team, but we showed up anyhow," Clark said. "I never had anybody to take me under their wings. Mays, Bonds, those guys were gone. It was just, 'Here guys, go out and play.'"

Clark's Giants tenure ended following a season-ending knee injury in 1984 and a falling out with manager Frank Robinson. The club traded him to St. Louis for four players, including shortstop Jose Uribe. The trade was a bad one for the Giants, as only Uribe made a meaningful contribution for San Francisco.

Clark, on the other hand, propelled the Cardinals to two World Series appearances. In his first playoff series against the Dodgers in 1985, he hit .381 against the Dodgers and clubbed a three-run, ninth-inning homer that clinched the pennant for St. Louis.

"It was the most wonderful feeling in the world," Clark said. "It did so much for me, my team, my manager, the owner, and the fans. It did so much and meant so much to fans in San Francisco, for all the years I played with the Giants."

Clark hit a career-high 35 home runs and 106 RBIs in 1987 when the Cardinals won another pennant. But he tore ligaments in his right ankle three weeks before the 1987 playoffs, forcing him to miss the postseason. Teammate Ozzie Smith's remarks that Clark should have played anyway caused a public stir and preceded his departure from St. Louis.

During his career, Clark sparred with managers and teammates on several other occasions, sometimes because Clark felt they showed the wrong attitude or failed to approach the game properly. His comments often fell on unappreciative ears, like the time he encouraged the Padres' popular Tony Gwynn to hit more aggressively with men on base.

"Tony was a great player. I just wanted him to be better," Clark said. "It wasn't a knock against Tony, it was a challenge, because we were trying to win. That whole thing was blown out of proportion ... He took it personally."

Nor was Clark easy on himself. Following a hitless night during his stint with Boston, Clark destroyed a dugout toilet with his Louisville Slugger in Kansas City. The Royals sent him a bill for $760. After leaving the Cardinals, Clark would play five more seasons for the Yankees, Padres, and Red Sox, but he never stayed anywhere for long.

"Swings angry. Talks angry. Leaves angry. Next city," summarized *Sports Illustrated* columnist Rick Reilly in 1991. "Nobody wears out a front-office welcome faster than the continually furious Jack Clark, baseball's all-time league leader in boats rocked."

Clark retired after the 1992 season, a four-time All Star and veteran of 18 Major League campaigns. He hit .267 with 340 home runs and 1,180 RBIs for his career. During his final two years in Boston, Clark earned nearly $3 million per season. His baseball income allowed him to pursue an expensive passion beyond his playing days.

Clark formed his own Top Fuel drag racing team in 1989, hiring the famous Tom "Mongoose" McEwen as his driver. Clark's "Taco Bell Express" dragster could go from zero to 100 miles per hour in less than a second, and exceeded 300 mph at top speed.

"My father used to take me to racetracks in Southern California when I was a little kid," Clark said. "Six thousand horsepower gets in your blood a little bit. It was a great experience for me and for my family. I'm glad I was able to do that for my father and give him some enjoyment in life."

The expense ran into millions of dollars, and Clark fell nearly $7 million in debt in the summer of 1992. When he declared bankruptcy, Clark listed among his assets his collection of 18 cars, including a $717,000 Ferrari. But Clark says his lifestyle was not the problem.

"I didn't have financial problems. People ripped me off, and I fought back," Clark said. "I used something that the government makes available to us. I'm not the first athlete that financial guys ripped off. I chose not to stand there and eat it."

Clark earned his racing license and began driving his dragster himself at the Mile-High Nationals near Denver in 1994. Clark covered the quarter-mile distance in 5.566 seconds, with a top speed of 210 mph. In another race, Clark reached 297 mph.

Ironically, the high-speed accident that nearly killed Clark occurred not in a drag race, but after he returned to baseball.

❀ ❀ ❀ ❀ ❀ ❀

Clark took the field with the Dodgers on Opening Day in 2001. Remembering the many wounds the Ripper inflicted on Los Angeles as a player, Dodgers fans greeted him with deafening boos.

"It made me feel great. Nobody had a bigger smile than me," Clark said. "'You guys hate me, I hate you even worse.' There were 55,000 of them booing me, and one of me smiling. When I had their hatred, I knew I had them. It was a tribute of the impact I've had, that I hurt them and damaged them."

The Dodgers handed Clark a dilemma when they offered him a position as hitting coach. Many have crossed the Giants-Dodgers divide before, but Clark fiercely believes in loyalty between players and their teams, and even former players and their former teams. Yet the Giants and Cardinals had nothing for him. He took the Los Angeles job.

"I felt like a traitor," Clark said. When Giants fans at Pac Bell Park told him he shouldn't have done it, he agreed with them. "You're right, I shouldn't have," he answered. "But I'm being made to. I have to do it."

Many Dodgers hitters believe they benefited from Clark's guidance during his Los Angeles tenure.

"He was a great hitting coach," said Los Angeles slugger Shawn Green. "He helped me a lot. He's someone you can rely on when you're struggling, and he helps you with your confidence."

Longtime Dodger Eric Karros agreed. "He always had something good to say," Karros said. "He could speak from experience, because he played the game and was on both ends of the spectrum, on top of the game and then when he went to Boston and had some struggles there. He could relate. He remembers how difficult it is to play this game."

Clark liked working with the hitters, though he never resolved his inner conflict that came from helping an organization he instinctively despises.

"I didn't like them when I was a Giant, and I don't like them now," Clark said of the Dodgers. "They think everyone else is stupid, and they always have a chip on their shoulder. That's what bothers all the other organizations and gives you that attitude to beat them."

Clark's collision occurred the day before Los Angeles' first game in 2003. Clark was riding his motorcycle to Bank One Ballpark in Phoenix for the Dodgers' final preseason workout.

Traffic was light on the Sunday morning. Clark rode his Chopper without a helmet, as Arizona law permits. He was about to exit the freeway for the ballpark when he saw one speeding car smash another in the car-pool lane far on his left. The front car's driver hit the brakes, and the back car hit it again, this time on the side.

"The car spins like a helicopter blade," Clark said. "In two seconds it's all the way across five lanes, in front of me, still spinning around. I've got a couple seconds to make a decision. I know I'm going to hit this car head on. There's no place for me to go. As the car spun perpendicular with me, I hit the throttle and tried to drive around it. I saw a small window of opportunity as a professional race car driver to try to get out of danger. I thought I'd pull it off, too. I don't remember anything from there, until waking up in hospital and somebody stitching up my head."

Clark suffered a severe concussion, a gash to his forehead, six broken ribs, a dislocated collarbone, and ligament damage in his right hand.

"I was hurt pretty bad," said Clark, the father of four. "If I had a helmet on, that would have helped me, but I didn't. I look at it like this: I'm still here because God wants me to be here. He's still got something planned for me, and I feel really good about that... Maybe it was for my children."

Months passed before Clark was able to fully return to work. Meanwhile, the Dodgers began the season with a terrible offensive drought. In Clark's first two seasons with Los Angeles, the team used strong pitching to compensate for its low run support, contending for the Wild Card berth both years. But in 2003, the Dodgers posted the worst offensive numbers in the National League, dead last in runs, home runs, hits, walks, and batting average.

Recovering from his accident, Clark wasn't even present for much of the slump. After he got back on his feet, though, the Dodgers fired him on August 3.

Clark believes the management made him a scapegoat, even though he made the most of a roster filled with "underachievers who make too much money." But he thinks the team's results in 2004 show how valuable he was to the offense.

"Look at Adrian Beltre's turnaround. I changed his stance and got him to square back up," Clark said. "Green hasn't been the same since I left. I get up there, and he hits 49 and 42 home runs. Now he's on pace to hit 20 again. To me, I was worth all the money in the world for that one guy alone."

Clark became the manager of a spectacularly bad Minor League team in 2004. After a last-place finish and a 33-57 record in 2003, the [Columbia] Mid-Missouri Mavericks of the Frontier League looked to Clark for a much-needed boost. No one imagined the carnage that awaited.

The 2004 Mavericks lost games on wild pitches, errant throws and pickoffs. When the pitching held, the offense disappeared. When the hitters hit, the pitching imploded.

"We made more mistakes than humanly possible. I saw things I've never seen in baseball before," Clark said. "When you're down by eight runs in the first or second inning every night, it's hard to manage."

After the Mavericks lost 26 of their first 30 games, Clark stepped aside as manager to become the team's director of baseball operations. In part, the move allowed Clark to spend more time with his family after his father was diagnosed with cancer. It also gave him latitude to shake up the roster: Clark thought little of the previous player procurement officer's work.

Clark endured two and a half years as the Dodgers' hitting coach.
Los Angeles Dodgers photo

"He left the organization hanging with a bad mix of people that didn't have baseball skills," Clark said. "I wish the team I was able to put together was there from the start. They are playing better now."

Clark also became the hitting coach of the first-year McKinney (Texas) Marshals, and he split his time between the two teams for the rest of the 2004 season. The Marshals proved far more competitive, winning their four-team division of the independent Texas Collegiate League with 33 wins and 19 losses. Clark later became manager of the Springfield Sliders.

Clark's health has mostly returned, though he still has occasional lapses of balance, and he can't throw the ball like he once did. He even gets back on a motorcycle once in a while. But how long will Jack the Ripper, once among the game's most imposing hitters, remain in the minor leagues?

"Jack Clark is different in my eyes than any other hitting coach I've ever had," said Marquis Grissom, the Giants' former center fielder who spent two years with Clark in Los Angeles. "I think a lot of clubs out there are just missing out. The way he loves to work at the game is unbelievable."

Clark helped Grissom extend his career by becoming more of a "gap to gap" hitter, the center fielder said. Grissom hit .221 in 2001 when Clark arrived in Los Angeles, .277 in 2002, and .300 as a Giant in 2003.

"I really don't understand why he's not in the big leagues," Grissom said. "Minor leagues, that's good, but Jack Clark is a big league hitting coach."

Clark agrees, even though he doesn't miss his last big league job.

"The brainwashing that goes on with the Dodger blue is kind of sickening," Clark said. "I never threw up, but sometimes I sure wanted to."

JOHNNIE LeMASTER

BONES, BOOS, AND GOD

Johnnie LeMaster feels lucky to be alive. In 1978, the Giants shortstop was back home in Kentucky, driving over a bridge on a February night, when a drunk driver smashed into his vehicle head-on. While LeMaster and the other driver were not hurt, the accident changed his life.

"I should have been killed and wasn't. That made me seriously think about the afterlife. Is there a Heaven or Hell?" he said. "The next two days I studied the Bible, and I wanted to know the truth. I didn't want someone's opinion."

Now, LeMaster devotes his life to Christianity and helping others. When he isn't busy running two sporting goods stores he owns and coaching the local college's baseball team, he teaches Bible study. LeMaster, a leader at the Paintsville Church of Christ, preaches at a local prison every Monday night for two hours. Every summer, he travels to Peru to do missionary work. His congregation joins a group of doctors as they dispense free medical check-ups to the poor and teach them the Gospels.

"If you ever want to have your spiritual life uplifted, I recommend going on a medical mission trip. You find out how fortunate you really are. We here in the United States are spoiled to death," he said. "These people don't have roofs over their homes. They have dirt floors. We're sitting there having Bible study, and chickens and ducks are walking between my legs."

For 12 years, LeMaster's job was to make sure groundballs didn't go through his legs.

Tall and lean, LeMaster was solid defensively as he patrolled the infield for the Giants for 11 years, from 1975 to 1985. During his six years as a starting shortstop, LeMaster averaged 22 errors a year, no small feat at Candlestick Park, where groundballs took funny hops off the rocky field.

"The wind would blow the top layer off the dirt during the game. There were craters all over the place," he recalled.

*Though better known for his glove, Johnnie LeMaster
hit an inside-the-park home run in his first Giants at-bat.*
© S.F. Giants

Nicknamed "Bones" for his wiry frame, LeMaster was a brilliant shortstop with great range, said former Giants closer Greg Minton.

"I'm a sinker-ball pitcher, and 'Bonesy' could get anything and everything," Minton said. "He was more valuable than anyone ever knew. He was one of the greatest ballplayers defensively."

Dave Heaverlo, a former Giant reliever, agreed. "Defensively, LeMaster was very reliable and had a cannon for an arm," he said.

LeMaster struggled offensively, however, and was booed heavily by Giants fans. His career-high batting average was .254 in 1979. His best offensive season was 1983, when manager Frank Robinson made LeMaster the team's leadoff hitter. That year, LeMaster stole 39 bases while batting .240 with six home runs and 30 RBIs.

"Hitting in the leadoff spot was a dream come true," said LeMaster, a career .222 hitter. "Frank Robinson said I had a green light, and it paid off. You don't steal 39 bases without being able to run a little bit and having a little bit of smarts."

LeMaster is also the 43rd player ever to hit a home run in his first Major League at-bat. It was his first day in the big leagues. He, Minton and a third Minor League player were September call-ups, arriving at Candlestick 30 minutes before a game against the Dodgers. With a full house in the stands, LeMaster thought to himself, "This is great. Here I am, and I get to watch a big league game from a dugout."

In the second inning, however, Giants shortstop Chris Speier pulled a hamstring running to first on a grounder, and manager Bill Rigney told LeMaster to take over at shortstop. With his late arrival, LeMaster didn't have a chance to take batting or infield practice before the game, so he was eager to get acclimated to the field and toss a few throws to first base between innings.

His teammates, however, had other ideas for the rookie. They hid both LeMaster's glove and cap in the dugout. It took him a while to find them.

"By the time I had gotten out on the field, the pitcher had warmed up. I didn't get to throw the ball to first base," he said. "Luckily, no one on the Dodgers hit it to me."

In LeMaster's first at-bat, he smacked an inside-the-park home run against Don Sutton.

"He throws me a curveball, and I miss by three feet. He throws me another curveball, and I miss it by about four feet. Why he threw me a fastball on the third pitch, I don't know, but I hit a line drive to center field," LeMaster said. "It hit a seam on the Astroturf, bounced straight over the top of the center fielder's head, and rolled all the way to the wall. That was the fastest I ever ran, and I slid into home."

Years later, LeMaster got Sutton to sign the home-run ball, which he's kept as a memento. "I was walking on air, thinking, 'This is easy,'" said LeMaster, recalling his first game as a Giant. "It didn't turn out to be that easy."

Perhaps embittered by the freezing temperatures at Candlestick and years of losing, fans took their anger out on LeMaster.

"I popped off to the newspaper and said things about the ballpark I shouldn't have said, and the fans didn't like it too much. I made a couple of errors, and they started booing me," LeMaster recalled. "My wife said, 'You should just wear 'Boo' in the back of your jersey.'"

LeMaster liked the idea and talked clubhouse manager Eddie Logan into stitching the jersey up. One day in 1979, he took the field with "Boo" on the back of his uniform. When the inning ended, LeMaster was handed his regular jersey, and general manager Spec Richardson fined him $500. "The fans loved it. The media loved it, and that's why they call me 'Boo,'" he said.

Since retiring, LeMaster has come back to San Francisco twice for on-field ceremonies, once as part of the All-Decade Team of the '80s and again for the last game at Candlestick Park in 1999. Both times, he was showered with boos. Bones doesn't mind. In some ways, he brought it onto himself for wearing "Boo" on his uniform, he said.

"I guess any athlete would want fans to cheer and clap for them. They die for a standing ovation," he said. "It was the other gambit for me."

Minton, who was also booed by Giants fans at the end of his tenure in San Francisco, bristled at the reaction LeMaster received during the on-field ceremony for the All-Decade Team. Minton was standing on the mound, and when LeMaster was announced and ran to the shortstop position, the fans booed him. Minton ran to LeMaster immediately and gave him a high-five as a show of support.

"It's tremendously unfair," Minton said of the fans' reaction. "Bonesy had trouble hitting, but that man can play defense. He has the respect of anyone who ever played with him."

His teammates used to tell the media, through newspapers and radio, that it was wrong for fans to pick on LeMaster, recalled former Giants pitcher Bob Knepper.

"People don't realize what his wife feels like in the stands," Knepper said. "Yet through all that, I never heard Johnny bad-mouth anybody or rip the fans. He maintained a sense of humor. How he was able to maintain that is a real indication of his character."

LeMaster was released by the Giants in 1985 when Jose Uribe took over at shortstop. LeMaster bounced from Cleveland to Pittsburgh that year, then retired. After a year off in 1986, Oakland Athletics manager Tony LaRussa called him in 1987 and asked him if he'd like to make a comeback as a utility infielder and backup to shortstop Alfredo Griffin, who suffered from back troubles.

LeMaster spent half the year with the A's, rooming with rookie Mark McGwire. "I was sitting on the bench as a piece of insurance," said LeMaster, who played in 20 games, and had three hits in 24 at-bats before retiring for good at age 33.

*LeMaster owns two sporting goods stores
and volunteers his time as an evangelist.*
Photo by Matt Johanson

After retiring, he went home to Paintsville, a five-square-mile city in eastern Kentucky with about 4,000 residents. In 1989, he opened two sporting goods stores—named Johnnie LeMaster Sports Center—in Paintsville and nearby Pikeville. He also entered local politics, serving two terms, for a total of four years, as a Paintsville city councilman. His proudest achievement on the council was getting approval to update and rebuild the city's rundown parks and recreational facilities without having to raise taxes.

"We found the money to get baseball fields, basketball courts, and tennis courts up to par, where kids feel proud to play in them," he said.

LeMaster coached Little League for seven years, and now coaches college players. For more than a decade, LeMaster has managed the Pikeville College Bears, compiling a 280-244 record. He won his league's Coach of the Year award in 1997. However, the 2004 season was lost to a rash of season-ending injuries.

The team's four best pitchers got hurt, two of them requiring Tommy John arm surgery. Four position players also got hurt. With only nine available players on the team, LeMaster had to forfeit most of the games in 2004 and ended the season 3-21.

"We've had good seasons every year up until this year," LeMaster said. "It's the worst year I've ever had, the most injury-prone year. It was like somebody was chopping down trees, one after another. We had only two pitchers left."

On a typical weekday, LeMaster wakes up at 8 A.M. and drives the 40 miles to Pikeville College to cut the grass and make sure the field is ready for practice or the game later that day. Now in his late 50s, LeMaster doesn't look like he's aged since his playing days. "Throwing batting practice everyday keeps you in shape," he said.

LeMaster's wife Debbie helps him run the sporting goods stores by handling the office paper work. His stores are big: 4,000 square feet in Pikeville and 3,000 square feet in Paintsville. He has eight full-time employees and 16 part-timers. They sell shoes and high-end equipment for baseball, basketball, football and tennis, everything except hunting and fishing. LeMaster said he focuses on high-end equipment to differentiate himself from Wal-Mart and Kmart, which sell lower-end goods.

"The large discount stores are pretty good competition, but we carry the top of the line baseball stuff for college and high school players, like your Rawlings baseball gloves. They come in looking for things they cannot get at Wal-Mart," he said.

One other advantage is that his stores are well-stocked with Nike shoes. Nikes aren't sold at the discount stores he competes with, he said. He spends a considerable amount of time meeting with sales representatives from shoemakers Nike, Adidas, and Reebok, ordering products six months in advance.

LeMaster entered the sporting goods business in 1989 by taking over a store that was going out of business. He has since made it profitable.

"It's been very good to me," he said. "It's paid a lot of bills."

He still keeps in touch with former Giants teammates, such as reliever Gary Lavelle, who lives in Virginia, and starting pitcher Atlee Hammaker, who lives in Tennessee. Once a year, they have a reunion and spend time with each other. Despite the boos, LeMaster said he has fond memories of his time in San Francisco. His favorite years were '78 and '82 when the Giants contended for the division title, but admits every year was fun.

"I wish I could relive and do them all over again," he said. "You spend 13 years in one organization, you get fond of it."

LeMaster, an elder at his church, said he will continue to devote his life to helping others because of two verses in the Bible, located at the end of the Book of Matthew, Chapter 28, which begins: *"Go ye therefore, and teach all nations, baptising them in the name of the Father, and of the Son, and of the Holy Ghost...."*

That's why he regularly teaches Bible study to prisoners and to the poor in Peru, and one time, to residents in Panama. And that's why he served on the City Council from 1991 to 1994: to make the community a better place to live.

"I want to do what is right, what God wants me to do. So far, I feel like I've done that," he said. "You have to keep to priorities. We're going to be here a short time. You try to leave it a better place."

Today, LeMaster is still an elder for the Paintsville Church of Christ. In 2008, he was added to AT&T Park's Giants Wall of Fame, a tribute to the team's greatest players. LeMaster's plaque highlights his ten years as a Giant, his excellent defense, and his record 1,479 putouts at shortstop.

MARK DAVIS

TEACHING BABY 'BACKS THE ABCs

Mark Davis spent 18 years on the mound staring at a catcher's mitt. In 2004, he spent much of his time staring at a computer screen, developing game plans for his young pitchers and writing critiques of their performances.

The former Giants pitcher traded in his baseball glove for a clipboard and laptop computer when he became a pitching coach in the Arizona Diamondbacks organization in 1999. After four years of coaching minor leaguers and a stint as bullpen coach for the Major League club, he was promoted to pitching coach for the last-place D-Backs midway through the 2004 season, after manager Bob Brenly and pitching coach Chuck Kniffin were fired.

Arizona, which began a youth movement in 2003 when Davis was bullpen coach, relied on even more inexperienced minor leaguers in 2004 when a rash of injuries derailed the season. With only three veterans on his staff, Davis spent much of his time teaching his young pitchers. It helped that Davis had worked with most of them before in the minor leagues, making their transition to the major leagues easier.

"When our young guys came up, it's guys I worked with or had seen for years. They said, 'Ah, MD is here.' It's a familiar face. They feel comfortable talking to me," said the 1989 Cy Young Award winner. "I didn't need to learn them. They didn't need to learn me. They knew the way they acted in front of me was fine."

That year, Davis arrived at the ballpark six hours before game time, pecking away at the computer. He reviewed scouting reports, analyzed pitcher and hitter statistics, and developed a generic game plan for all the pitchers, then a specific game plan for the day's starting pitcher.

After games, Davis got on the computer again, writing a review of his young starters' performances, focusing on their mechanics, their body language, and

Mark Davis pitched his best games against the Dodgers.
© S.F. Giants

their aggressiveness. After Randy Johnson, Arizona's four starters averaged about two years of Major League service.

"I critique their overall game, and what I see each inning," he said. "I give them that, so they can remember what they did, look at what I thought, then we talk about it."

An East Bay native, Davis grew up hating the Dodgers. In the 1970s, Los Angeles dominated the rivalry with the likes of Ron Cey and Steve Garvey. Davis wanted to take the mound at Candlestick Park and beat the Dodgers himself.

In 1983, his dream came true.

After years of braving the Candlestick winds as a fan, Davis was on the mound in a Giants uniform at the 'Stick, starting against Tommy Lasorda's division-leading team. He was a 22-year-old left-handed rookie. His parents and friends watched from the stands.

That Saturday afternoon in July, he shut out the enemy, 8-0, scattering seven hits for his first victory as a Giant. Los Angeles mounted one feeble scoring threat with two singles with one out in the fourth, but Davis squelched it when Steve Yeager grounded into an inning-ending double play.

In mid-September, Davis outdid himself, blanking the Dodgers again at Candlestick, this time a 1-0 victory, giving up just two hits on eight strikeouts. Two weeks later, he faced Los Angeles a third time at Dodgers Stadium on NBC's Saturday "Game of the Week," and nearly shut out Los Angeles a third straight time, going 8 1/3 innings before giving up a run in a 4-1 victory. In three starts, the rookie outdueled the Dodgers' Jerry Reuss, Fernando Valenzuela, and Burt Hooton.

Davis, a two-time All-Star, enjoyed his Dodger-killing activities during his five Giants seasons.

"The Giants-Dodgers rivalry meant a lot to me growing up," said the baby-faced Davis, still youthful-looking in his early 50s. "I always pitched well against the Dodgers, either as a starter or in the bullpen. To play for the Giants and beat the Dodgers three times, twice on shutouts. To me, that's a big deal."

Davis, who lives in Scottsdale, Arizona, with his wife and four children, is the first to admit he had great and awful years. In a career spanning parts of 18 seasons, he racked up a 51-84 record, with a 4.17 ERA and 96 saves. He believes his up-and-down career gave him the wisdom to help younger players.

"I've done everything: I've been an Opening Day starter, a closer, and everything in the middle. I've also been the pitcher they didn't want there, the 12th man on an 11-man staff," he said. "I've been hurt. I've been operated on. I've had to totally redo my mechanics. I've faced everything you can face as a pitcher. So when I talk to a guy, I know what it's like. I've been there."

Davis, 6-foot-4 and 205 pounds, threw one of the best curveballs in the 1980s, a beautiful, rainbow breaking ball. For batters on both sides of the plate, it was a nasty pitch that dropped down hard. He complemented his curve with a sizzling fastball that reached 93 mph. When Davis was on, he was unhittable.

One of Davis' most memorable Giants moments came in 1985, when he pitched an inning of relief against the New York Mets, and threw all curve balls, 23 to be exact. Davis tried to shake them off, but catcher Steve Nicosia kept calling for it.

"They're not hitting it, so just keep throwing it," Nicosia told the pitcher. Davis retired the side, 1-2-3.

Davis' career began with the Philadelphia Phillies. A first-round draft pick, he reached the majors in his second season of pro ball. His first game as a major leaguer was at Candlestick Park.

"It was cool sitting in the bullpen at Candlestick, going, 'You know what? I always said it's got to be warmer on the field when I was sitting in the stands.' And it wasn't any warmer out there," said Davis, laughing. "But it was neat to go through the day in a stadium I was at as a kid. My parents were there. It was special."

While growing up in Livermore, Davis' father dragged him to the Oakland Coliseum to watch the Athletics play. But in the late '70s, as soon as he learned to drive, he drove to Candlestick to watch the Giants instead. He was a pitcher for Livermore's Granada High School and Chabot College in nearby Hayward. He preferred the National League because pitchers were allowed to hit.

His favorite players, Vida Blue and Jack Clark, later became his teammates. As a teen, Davis once met Clark on the field at Candlestick. It was a pre-game ceremony, and Clark awarded plaques to honor Bay Area high school all-stars. "He shook my hand. It was a thrill," he said.

Two years later, while bouncing between Triple-A, the Phillies, and the disabled list, Davis was traded to the Giants, along with Mike Krukow and C.L. Penigar. In return, Philadelphia received Joe Morgan and Al Holland.

Davis, who considered Krukow a mentor, started 20 games for the Giants in 1983 and finished the season a respectable 6-4 with a 3.49 ERA. Perhaps because of his superb performances against the Dodgers, he was rewarded with the Opening Day start in 1984. "That was a big deal," Davis said. "Huey Lewis sang the national anthem. I thought it was cool because I liked him."

But Davis lost the game and had a disastrous year, posting a 5-17 record and a 5.36 ERA.

During the next two years, Davis worked almost exclusively out of the bullpen. In 1985, Davis broke the all-time appearance record for a left-handed pitcher, with 77, and was the first Giant reliever to reach more than 100 strikeouts in a season, with 131.

He never reached his potential as a Giant and was traded midway through the 1987 season, part of a seven-player trade that helped catapult the Giants into the National League Championship Series that year. The Giants received starter Dave Dravecky, reliever Craig Lefferts, and outfielder Kevin Mitchell for Davis,

Davis became the Arizona Diamondbacks' pitching coach.
Photo by Wylie Wong

third baseman Chris Brown, and pitchers Keith Comstock and Mark Grant.

Davis remembers the trade with humor. That night, he had just returned to the team hotel in Chicago when his phone rang. It was Doc Mattei, the Padres' traveling secretary, introducing himself.

"Who? What?" Davis said.

"So you haven't heard?" Mattei asked.

"Heard what?" Davis answered.

"I'll talk to you later," the secretary replied, and hung up.

"So I figured, 'OK, I must be going to the Padres," Davis said.

After the trade, Davis blossomed into an overpowering All-Star closer for San Diego. In 1988, he was 5-10 with a 2.01 ERA with 28 saves. In 1989, the year he won the Cy Young Award, he was 4-3, with a 1.85 ERA and 44 saves.

"I did the same thing in San Diego that I was doing with the Giants, except I was doing it in a different inning span, and that's why I had more notoriety," Davis said. "In San Diego, if I pitched in the seventh or eighth inning, sometimes I finished the game. I had the opportunity to pitch late in the game and to pitch to right-handers. Before, with the Giants, I wouldn't finish the game. They'd let someone else pitch the ninth."

As for his Cy Young season, everything just clicked from day one and it kept on clicking, he said. "I had a couple of quick saves and had 13 in the first month. It was a snowball thing. Any time I went out there, I either struck out four guys in an inning and a third, or if I needed help, I had a line drive that was hit right at somebody."

That off-season, he signed one of the richest free agent contracts for a reliever at that time, a four-year, $13 million contract with Kansas City. But he faltered as the Royals' closer, going 2-7 with a 5.11 ERA and six saves in 1990. Arm injuries cut short his career in the '90s as he bounced from Atlanta, Florida, and San Diego. After being out of baseball for two years, he made a last comeback attempt in 1997 with the Milwaukee Brewers, where he pitched in 19 games and recorded his 1,000th career strikeout.

"At one point, I felt I had a Velcro thing on my hat, and whoever I played for, I just stuck their logo on," he joked.

After four years working with Minor League pitchers in the Diamondbacks' organization, Davis became bullpen coach for Brenly, his former battery mate in San Francisco.

Many Diamondbacks pitchers, coached by Davis in the minor leagues, credited him with helping them make the big leagues and succeeding. Webb, who was 10-9 with a 2.84 ERA in his first full season in 2003, said he grew leaps and bounds under Davis' tutelage a year earlier in Double-A.

"He helped me out so much in Double-A, mechanically and mentally," said Webb, who finished third in Rookie of the Year balloting. "He knew what type of pitcher I am. I'm not going to blow a 95 mph fastball past somebody. I will rely on my movement and location to get guys out. When he wants to get a point across, he gets it across in a good way."

Davis recalls Webb getting upset in Double-A after giving up several ground-ball hits in an inning. "I told him, 'They've all been groundballs that just happen to get through. So don't worry about it,'" Davis told Webb. "If you get groundballs, that's what we want to see. More times than not, you're going to win."

In the 2003 season, with so many young pitchers in the bullpen like Oscar Villarreal, Stephen Randolph, and Jose Valverde, Davis said he tried to teach them lessons that took him years to learn as a pitcher.

"Some of them throw hard in the bullpen until they go in. I tell them, 'Don't waste your bullets.' Bullets in April may take away from August and September. And in August and September, guys who haven't done it before will say, 'Oh, I know what you mean,'" Davis said. "If you can save three to four pitches every time you warm up, that adds up to one or two more appearances in September. And that could be the difference if we can make it to the playoffs or not."

Former teammates called Davis, "Goofy," and the nickname stuck. Diamondbacks pitchers said he played practical jokes all the time, from wearing Hillbilly teeth to giving players pens and cigarette lighters that shock people trying to use them.

"He's just hyper 24/7. He's always in a good mood. I've never seen him in a bad mood," Webb said. "He's always playing practical jokes."

Diamondback closer Matt Mantei said he appreciated the laid back atmosphere in the bullpen. "He's a lot of fun to be around. He keeps the bullpen loose. It's great because we have a stressful job. You can't get too tense or nervous," Mantei said. "He knows we're not going to succeed every time out. It's big for us to have someone down there who's been a warrior, who's had a lot of success, but also battled through some hard times."

Davis said it's not healthy for bullpens to be too rigid or tense. "Some fans might look at us and think we're out of control, but you need to let off steam," he said. "I want everyone to know it's OK to joke around because there's no guarantee that you will pitch. If you know you're going to throw the seventh inning that night, then yeah, you can work yourself mentally to get ready for that. But it helps you be a more productive pitcher when you don't have to live and die with every inning."

The pitching staff said Davis' personality didn't change when he became pitching coach. He still kidded around. He just had less time to do it. As pitching coach, he spent half of batting practice sequestered in the bullpen, going over the game plan with the day's starting pitcher and catcher.

During games, Davis was hands-on. He charted the pitches, writing down the velocity and the type of pitches thrown. Sometimes he screamed at pitchers, "Too quick!" from the dugout if he felt they were rushing their delivery, resulting in bad mechanics and a bad pitch.

"He takes it harder than we do when we don't do so good," said reliever Mike Fetters.

For example, in one game, Webb rushed his delivery on two 3-2 counts earlier in the game. After reminding Webb to slow down in the dugout, the young right-hander made sure he stayed balanced and made a quality pitch the next time he had a 3-2 count, Davis recalled.

"I deal with the execution of making quality pitches. The more times you do that, your abilities will come through," he said. "Winning and losing games are a byproduct of pitching well. You can only pitch well by executing a pitch."

Davis plans to coach for the foreseeable future. Even though he no longer works for the Giants, he still has a soft spot for his boyhood team.

"If I can only go to one game a year, as a fan of baseball, it's the rivalry between the Giants and Dodgers," he said.

Since leaving the Diamondbacks after the 2005 season, Davis has coached for the Kansas City Royals organization. In 2011, he was the Royals' Minor League pitching coordinator. In 2012, he served as pitching coach for the Arizona League Royals, the team's rookie-league affiliate.

CHRIS BROWN

IRAQI ROAD WARRIOR

Chris Brown died on December 26, 2006 from injuries he sustained from a fire in his home in suburban Houston. He was 45. This chapter was written at the end of his first year as a Halliburton contractor in Iraq.

Dodging gunfire and explosions was not in Chris Brown's career plans, but the former Giant needed a job.

For years, Brown operated a crane for a construction business in Houston, but work dried up. So when government contractor Halliburton offered high-paying jobs to help rebuild war-torn Iraq, he signed up.

Brown, a Giant from 1984 to 1987, drives 18-wheel trucks to deliver fuel from one U.S. military base to another. With about 40 Halliburton workers killed in Iraq, he is well aware of the dangers he faces. Brown has been shot at, several times, by insurgents with rifles, mortars, and rocket-propelled grenades. But he has so far traversed through Iraq unscathed.

"I'm just a spontaneous type of person. Work slowed down, and I had the opportunity to come here," said Brown, in his early forties. "The Lord has blessed me that nothing has happened to me."

It's late July 2004, and Brown worked in Iraq for ten months. He had just returned to the Middle East after a two-week vacation with his wife Lisa, a flight attendant, and their two young children back home in Houston. He also took a side trip to attend a childhood friend's wedding and to see his oldest adult son in Los Angeles.

"It's going fine. I'm just getting back into the swing of things," he said of his return to Iraq. "It was wonderful to see my wife and family. We made a lot of good time together."

He works 12 hours a day, from 5 a.m. to 5 p.m., seven days a week. He wears a helmet and bulletproof vest while he makes his deliveries with a military escort.

Third baseman Chris Brown became an All-Star in 1986.
Brace Photo

Brown lives in a military base called Camp Cedar II at the Tallil Airbase, about 160 miles southeast of Baghdad. The heat reaches 130 degrees. But most of the time, he is somewhere with air conditioning, either in a truck or in a military building.

He shares a room with a close friend and neighbor from Houston who took a job with Halliburton at the same time he did. But he's also made many new friends who work for the company, which is delivering fuel, food, and other support services to U.S. troops in Iraq.

"I've met guys out here who live down the street from me that I didn't know. We've got different cultures, different nationalities from different parts of the United States," he said. "We make the best of it. We try to work, make money, and come home safe."

Brown, one of five children, grew up in South Central Los Angeles and played high school baseball with Darryl Strawberry at Crenshaw High School. His mom, Maggie Brown Hubbard, a nurse who raised all her children by herself, remembers Brown only needed three things to stay happy as a child: food, cartoons, and sports. "I'm going to be on TV and hit home runs," he told her while growing up.

Brown broke in with San Francisco as a September call-up in 1984 and showed the promise that made him a second-round pick in the 1979 draft. In 23 games that year, he hit .286, one home run and 11 RBIs in 84 at bats.

Brown became an All-Star in 1986, representing the Giants with Chili Davis and Mike Krukow at the midseason classic in the Houston Astrodome. Brown ripped a double and scored a run in two at-bats in the game. With a .317 average that year, Brown was among the National League leaders.

"I shortened my swing, changed my hitting stance, and saw the ball better," he said. "And for the majority of the season, I was seeing it like it was a beach ball."

When Brown became a big leaguer and an All-Star, Hubbard was ecstatic. "I was really proud," she said. "I always knew he was going to do something out of the ordinary, and I knew it was something in sports."

But Brown fell victim to a rash of injuries throughout his career. He missed 31 games in 1985 and 46 games in his All-Star year in 1986. That year, he needed shoulder surgery after a collision at the plate. Then one month into the 1987 season, Cardinals pitcher Danny Cox broke Brown's jaw with a fastball.

While some of his injuries were serious, he still had a reputation for begging out of games with minor injures that other players ignored. Teammates had hard feelings when Brown didn't play.

"I think everyone was disappointed when he didn't play as much as he could have because we were a better team when he played. He was very talented," said former Giants teammate Joel Youngblood. "As a teammate, I would want him in 150 games a year because of his tremendous ability. But we can't judge him."

The national media, however, judged Brown during the summer of 2004. In a story publicizing Brown's work in Iraq, *Sports Illustrated* called him the "softest player in the '80s" who now "has one of the hardest jobs of the 2000s." The magazine and news wire services recounted how teammates nicknamed him the "Tin Man," after the Wizard of Oz character who had no heart.

"Every time I got injured, it was because I played hard, and I don't regret it," Brown said. He also scoffed at the national media's portrayal of him as a loafer in the '80s who is somehow making up for it 20 years later by working in Iraq.

"Why do I have to justify myself? I came out here to work for the company to provide for my family. I'm not here to prove anything to anybody," he said. "My wife loves me, my family and my true friends love me, whether I played ball or not."

Brown was traded to San Diego in the summer of 1987, along with pitchers Mark Davis, Mark Grant, and Keith Comstock in exchange for Dave Dravecky, Kevin Mitchell, and Craig Lefferts.

Brown's career went on a downward spiral after the trade. He had a subpar second half for the Padres in 1987. Then in 1988, he played in only 80 games, batting .235 with two homers and 19 RBIs. He was traded to Detroit before the 1989 season, but was released a month into the season after hitting .193 in 17 games. His baseball career ended at age 27.

Brown takes it in stride that he didn't become the player others predicted he would become. Brown said simply making it to the big leagues was a dream come true. "I've seen a lot of guys never make it, not even for a cup of coffee," he said. "At least I can say I made it to the major leagues."

When Brown told his mother he was going to Iraq, she tried to change his mind. "He always wants to help someone," Hubbard said. "I said, 'You don't have to help them over there. There are so many people over here to be helped.' He said, 'Yes, but it's a different challenge, and I'm going to take it on.'"

The worst part, Brown said, is being away from his family. In October 2003, one month into his tour of duty in Iraq, he missed his daughter's birthday and his wedding anniversary. He also missed Christmas that year.

"I talked to my family on the phone. It was hard because I never had been away from them. It was depressing. There's no other word for it," he said.

At least Brown is eating well in Iraq. He may be in a war zone, but he's not stuck in the desert eating combat rations. The menu at the military bases' cafeterias include steak, hamburgers, tacos, and roast beef.

"We got the same kind of food you have back home," he said. "We are in a military base. We ain't missing no meals for nothing. We had shrimp and lobster last night."

During his off-hours, Brown keeps in touch with family and friends. He calls home and checks email. For entertainment, he can shoot pool, play table tennis, or go swimming. Some military bases also get concerts.

"We have our own little city built," he said. "It's not as bad as they say."

Brown, pictured with his wife, Lisa, took a
job driving trucks for Halliburton in Iraq.
Chris Brown family photo

Once in a while, he is woken up by the sound of mortars, but he feels safe in the military bases. Tomorrow morning, he'll deliver fuel to another military base, about 200 miles away. Despite the second-guessing over the merits of the war in Iraq back home, Brown believes the U.S. military is doing well in helping rebuild Iraq.

"If you came here in September [2003] and looked at it now, it's like a 180-degree turn. It's getting better," he said. "They're trying to get this country where it should be. It used to be that women had no rights here."

Insurgents in Iraq have become violent, but Brown has met some friendly Iraqis, too. He's talked to a few Iraqis who sell goods at or around military bases.

"They have guys selling goods there. It's really a friendly atmosphere when you do get to talk to them," Brown said. "The majority understand why we are here, and why the military are doing what they're doing."

Brown signed a one-year contract with Halliburton. His one year is up in two months, in late September. When he goes home after his contract is up, he can come back to Iraq on a month-by-month basis. He hasn't decided what he will do yet.

Brown has always wanted to get back into baseball in some capacity, either as a coach or in a front office job. With the media attention he's getting for working in Iraq, he's hopeful that a Major League team will give him a chance. But at the same time, he's not going to wait around, and expects to continue his work with Halliburton in Iraq.

"Right now, work over here is good. If my wife does not have a problem with it, and my kids don't have a problem, I will come back month to month," he said.

He will also consult with a higher source before making a final decision, said Brown, a devout Christian.

"I will let the Lord choose," he said. "I'm a different person than I was in 1986. I tried to do everything on my own then. Now I follow what the Lord tells me to do."

According to the *Associated Press*, Brown completed three one-year tours in Iraq before returning home to the United States during the summer of 2006.

MARK GRANT

"BE YOURSELF"

Winning makes it easy, broadcasters say. But when a team struggles, they have to get creative. Just ask Mark Grant, the one-time Giant who became a color commentator for San Diego Padres' television broadcasts.

Grant once pulled an amusing stunt when the Padres visited Milwaukee, where the Brew Crew's mascot Bernie Brewer slides into a vat of beer to celebrate every Milwaukee home run. When a Padre homered that evening, San Diego's TV viewers were surprised to see the lederhosen-clad mascot slide into the suds for the Brewers' opponents, only to discover that the man in the costume was none other than the Padres' beaming broadcaster Grant.

"Winning takes care of everything," Grant said. "Everybody's in a good mood, everyone's having a good year. When you're losing, first you have to remember you're trying to keep an audience. A nice compliment I received was an e-mail that said, 'We like to watch the Padres on TV, and we realize it's a bad year. One of the reasons we stay tuned is because you guys like to have fun, and you keep it fun and interesting.'"

Grant's seasons as a Padres' broadcaster have made him a celebrity in San Diego, though the former pitcher got his start in San Francisco after the Giants drafted him in 1981. He came up through the Giants farm system and played two and a half seasons with the Giants before the team dealt him to San Diego in 1987.

"I take a lot of pride in being a home-grown Giant, getting drafted by the Giants, coming through the chain, and making it to the big leagues," Grant said. "I was lucky to play with guys like [Mike] Krukow, [Duane] Kuiper, Bob Brenly, and Jack Clark. Those guys were awesome."

Grant helped lighten the mood on a team that lost 100 games in his rookie year, said Kuiper.

Pitcher Mark Grant entertained teammates with his sense of humor.
© S.F. Giants

"He was the greatest rookie in the history of the Giants franchise, not on what he did on the field, but how much fun he was in the dugout and in the clubhouse," Kuiper said. "He made a couple of rocky years with the Giants a lot more fun just because of how much he made us laugh and how much we made him laugh."

Former Giants broadcaster Hank Greenwald recalled a humorous incident from Grant's first Major League start against Cincinnati. The Reds took exception when Grant hit a batter with a pitch. Cincinnati's pitcher beaned Grant in retaliation when he later came to bat.

"The Giants came pouring out of dugout, and a brawl ensued," Greenwald said. "Grant was totally oblivious to all of this. You get hit with a pitch, you go to first base. He was trying to do that in the middle of two converging teams. 'Excuse me, pardon me, I'm trying to get through here.' He had no idea what all this commotion was about."

Grant's best year as a Giant came in 1987, even though the team traded him on July 4. The right-handed reliever had already pitched 61 innings with a 3.54 ERA.

The trade sent Grant, Mark Davis, Keith Comstock, and Chris Brown to the Padres, in exchange for Kevin Mitchell, Dave Dravecky, and Craig Lefferts. Grant missed the Giants' division title in 1987 and league championship in 1989, but harbors no resentment.

"I'm all for trying to better the ballclub," Grant said. "That's exactly what they wanted to do. [Giants general manager] Al Rosen pulled the right strings."

Grant played five more seasons for the Padres, Braves, Mariners, Astros, and Rockies. His best post-Giants year came with the Padres in 1989, when he won eight and lost two, pitching 116 innings with a 3.33 ERA.

Nearing the end of his playing career, Grant considered a future in the broadcast booth. After practicing some play-by-play from the dugout, Grant became a radio sports anchor and talk show host, and later won a job calling Padres games.

"I think the best thing is to be yourself," Grant said. "There's only one Vin Scully, there's only one Jon Miller. Don't try to be those guys, because there's only one Mark Grant.

"I want to be the guy sitting on the couch, with a cold beverage and a bowl of popcorn, having fun, trying to teach some baseball," Grant said. "I don't have a shtick or whatever. I just want to be that guy that people are comfortable listening to. The biggest compliment I get is when people say after meeting me, 'You sound the same on the air as you do in person.'"

Padres players and fans alike appreciate Grant's down-to-earth personality and positive outlook, said longtime Padres pitcher Trevor Hoffman.

"People like to feel like he's talking directly to them. He does a nice job of that," said Hoffman. "He's always been positive, and that's something refreshing

Grant (center) takes the airwaves with his fellow Padres broadcasters.
Photo by John Dunphy

from a player's perspective. He's very respectful of the players in here, and they respect him as a former player."

Grant and his wife Mary have three children and live near San Diego in the city of Alpine. Grant credits his wife for coping with his frequent absences when he travels with the Padres.

"My wife gets it," he said. "She comes from a military family. She realizes that my job entails me being away some of the time."

In addition to his broadcasting duties, Grant volunteers his time for the Children's Hospital Foundation of San Diego, the Cystic Fibrosis Foundation, East County Boys and Girls Club, and the Down Syndrome Association of San Diego.

Grant is one of many former Giants who made the transition from the playing field to the broadcast booth. The Twins' Dan Gladden, ESPN's Joe Morgan, Spanish language broadcaster Tito Fuentes, and the Giants' Kruk and Kuip are among the others.

"It just goes to show you, the Giants like to sign people with good personalities," laughed Grant.

GREG MINTON

THE MOON MAN COMETH

W hen Bay Area homeowners opened their front doors, the last person they expected to see was Greg Minton.

In 2004, the former Giants closer worked as a salesman for California Gunite & Pool Plastering, a swimming pool refurbishing company. When a pool owner called for an appointment, Minton went out to the house, took a look at the pool, and explained his company's services. He was surprised by the number of people who remembered him.

"I give my business card and they instantly do a double take. 'Are you? Did you ever? Are you the one who?'" Minton said. "I say, 'Yes, I used to play baseball,' and they want to talk about baseball for four hours and 10 minutes."

Minton, known as the zany "Moon Man" in his playing days, enjoys talking to fans about his baseball career. "It amazes me when people ask me if I remember the time there were two on and two out in the eighth inning and Steve Garvey was at bat," Minton said.

He always tells them, "'No sir. I pitched 700-something games. I can't remember every one of them.'"

He had moved from the Phoenix area to Walnut Creek after he and his wife divorced. He received a baseball pension, but took the pool job for some extra income. He made house calls in the morning and wrote up contracts and handled assorted paperwork in the afternoon.

"I was too young to do nothing," said Minton, now in his early 60s. "This is a job with flexibility, and I enjoy what I'm doing. I don't have to wear a suit and tie, and I can go hunting and play golf when I want to."

Minton, who threw a nasty sinkerball, was a workhorse in the Giants bullpen, saving 125 games over 13 years, from 1975 to 1987. He ranks fourth in saves for the San Francisco franchise, behind Robb Nen, Rod Beck, and Gary Lavelle, with whom he shared closing duties.

Greg Minton was one of best closers in the early 1980s.
© S.F. Giants

Minton was one of the National League's best relievers in the early '80s, saving at least 19 games each season between 1980 and 1984. He made the All-Star team in 1982, when he posted a 10-4 record, a 1.83 ERA and 30 saves in 123 innings pitched. That year, he appeared in a team-high 78 games. In 1983, he and Gary Lavelle became the first teammates to save 20 games for a National League team in the same season.

Minton loved the pressure of closing out games. "My adrenaline flowed. I craved it," he said.

He was released by the Giants during the 1987 season and was picked up by the Angels, where he was an effective reliever until he retired after the 1990 season at age 38. During his 16-year career, he had a 59-65 record, 3.10 ERA and 150 saves.

"Just shows you what sandpaper and Vaseline on a baseball will do," he joked.

Teammates say Minton was a hilarious, fun-loving free spirit who lived up to his Moon Man moniker. "It had to do with spacing out and being spacey," said former Giants pitcher Bob Knepper, adding that Triple-A manager Rocky Bridges gave Minton the nickname. "Greg definitely marches to the beat of his own drum."

Minton, who grew up surfing on Southern California beaches, once brought his stereo to the shower room and cranked up the music before a game he was going to start, Knepper recalled. "He had a stereo in the bathroom playing Pink Floyd. It's reverberating in there as he's psyching up."

He also listened to music during games he pitched in. During one game in Chicago's Wrigley Field, Minton hauled his stereo into the dugout, so he could listen to music after every inning he pitched. "[Manager] Bill Rigney sees Greg sitting there zoning out with headphones on in the dugout and spacing out," Knepper said. "Rigney was old-school, and he just couldn't figure it out."

Minton's laid-back approach to life helped him succeed as a relief pitcher, Knepper said. "He had great stuff, a great curveball. He wasn't a guy who would study hitters. He had the ability to be 100 miles away in the bullpen. He wasn't on edge. Then you put him in a ballgame, and he's ready to go."

Minton admits that his nickname is well deserved. "I had more fun than most people," he said. "I was a team practical jokester. I pulled stunts to keep people loose. I'm much looser than most guys. You have to be if you're a closer."

The Moon Man's personality kept the bullpen from stressing out, said former Giant reliever Dave Heaverlo. "He taught me to laugh at myself. Some guys sit down and stay intense. As a reliever, you can't do that or you can have ulcers and go nuts."

Heaverlo added that Minton was one of the most unique and most bizarre characters he ever played with. "Had he not been a ballplayer, he would have been a disc jockey or door man for a topless bar somewhere," Heaverlo declared. "He had a real zest for life."

Minton never expected to become a baseball player. In 1970, when the United States was still knee-deep in the Vietnam War, a college friend ran up to Minton and told him, "You just got drafted."

"I went ballistic," recalled Minton, who told his friend, "I have a deferment. I am taking 15 units. I am not going into the Army."

"No, you dumbshit," his friend told him. "You got drafted by the Kansas City Royals."

Minton's main focus was surfing while growing up in Solana Beach, California, near San Diego. He never considered himself an athlete. He just played baseball because all his friends played.

"First thing I did was go to my atlas," he said, after getting drafted by the Royals. "I couldn't find a beach anywhere close to Kansas City. I thought, 'This isn't working.'"

Three years later, Minton—who threw a straight mid-90s fastball—was traded to the Giants organization. Minton developed his sinker while pitching batting practice during Spring Training in the late '70s. He was recovering from knee surgery at the time. The coaching staff didn't want Minton's arm to atrophy, so they told him to toss 20 minutes of batting practice.

Because of his surgically repaired knee, Minton took a shorter stride than normal and tried to throw fastballs to catcher Mike Sadek. The result was a fast pitch that sank straight down. By taking the short stride, he had accidentally discovered how to throw a sinker.

"Mike takes his mask off and says, 'Moonie, what are you doing? Throw it straight. I don't want to be here either, so quit screwing around,'" Minton recalled. "I wasn't meaning to do it."

Minton and Lavelle used to protect themselves from Candlestick's howling winds by hanging out in the sauna in the Giants locker room during games. They watched the game on closed-circuit television.

"He and I would go there in the sixth inning and get a little sweat working," Minton said.

When the later innings arrived, Minton and Lavelle would wait inside the stadium, inside the big tunnel doors that opened out to the Giants bullpen in right field.

"Why freeze?" he said. "We would stay in the tunnel doors, and when the phone rang, Lavelle and I were warm and toasty. Everyone else had purple fingers."

Some Candlestick fans got a little rowdy because of alcohol consumption. Minton remembers cops in riot gear, wearing padded vests and helmets, would spill out on the field after the games. While waiting, the police entertained the bullpen with crime stories.

Minton's career highlight was the 1982 All-Star Game. When Minton found out he made the National League team during a game against the Mets at Shea Stadium, he immediately called his father and told him to fly to Montreal for the game. Minton never made the all-league team in high school, so this was a big deal.

"My dad is my best friend, and one of my fondest memories is getting my dad in the locker room," he recalled. "I'm lockering next to Pete Rose and he says, 'Mr.

Minton, if we had your son, we'd be 25 games out in front.'"

In the eighth inning, after Fernando Valenzuela got two outs, Dodger manager Tommy Lasorda brought in Minton to get the third out.

"I don't remember touching the ground. The catcher comes out and says, 'Keep throwing that shit you've thrown to us all year, and we'll get out of this thing,'" said Minton, who got the third out on a grounder to shortstop Ozzie Smith.

After retiring from baseball in 1990, Minton took the next five years off to raise his children, then returned to baseball as a Minor League manager and coach from 1995 to 2000.

In his first two years, Minton returned to his Texas hometown to manage the Lubbock Crickets in an independent league, winning a championship in 1995. He not only managed, but he also built the team by recruiting players who were released by other organizations. "We gave them another opportunity," he said.

Then he rejoined the Angels organization, serving as pitching coach in their Minor League organization. The most difficult part of coaching was winning the respect of his players who knew of his "Moon Man" reputation, Minton said.

"My reputation was the team flake. I was the crazy man. I went into it wondering if anyone was going to listen to me, and they listened to me," he said.

Minton imparted his wisdom to pitching prospects, including Jarrod Washburn and Scott Schoeneweis, who eventually made the big league club. He taught the youngsters about pitching techniques and the mental aspects of the game that he wished he knew while starting out.

"What people didn't realize was that I didn't make All-League. I was never a superstar in high school," he said. "It was my perseverance. I had to learn the hard way to get people out."

Minton loved coaching and found it rewarding, but retired in 2000 after tiring of the tough travel schedule. He had spent nearly three decades traveling with Major and Minor League teams. A father of five, Minton wanted to spend time with his youngest children before they graduated from high school.

"Someone paid me to throw things at people. What job is better in the world, right?" he said. "I still love the game. I'm done traveling."

Minton is willing to travel, however, if it means he can take two-week trips to Arizona, Texas, and other states to hunt with his bow.

He started hunting in 1990, but realized quickly that shooting antelope and elk with guns and binoculars was too easy. "There's nothing like a 600-pound elk thrashing trees and snorting snot and coming at you when you've got a stick and string in your hands," he said.

Hunting is more than simply killing an animal, he said. As an archer, Minton has to get close enough to the animal to get a good shot. Sometimes he moves just three feet an hour as he carefully eyes his prey. He also has to take into account the wind, the trees, and other terrain. Minton and his companions camp out at night, then continue hunting during daylight.

"I've gone hunting and not shot anything and still had the greatest time," he said.

Minton also keeps his hands in baseball. He plays in weekend softball tourna-

*Minton, forced by injuries to pitch as a lefty
in his retirement, delivers to a fantasy camp batter.*
Photo by Matt Johanson

ments—"beer leagues," as he calls it. Minton, who is ambidextrous, can only throw left-handed now. After three surgeries on his right shoulder, he can't raise his right arm.

He's made appearances for the Giants over the years. He spends one week a year in Arizona at the Giants fantasy baseball camp. He also served breakfast and talked to fans who attended the 2004 slumber party event at the Giants ballpark, where they pitched tents and camped out on the field overnight.

Minton said he had a fun time at the slumber party, where he signed autographs and bonded with the children. He also had nice chats with the kids' parents and grandparents who rooted for Minton in the '70s and '80s. Always on the lookout for good camping gear for his hunting trips, he even got a chance to check out some new tents at the event.

"I go there as the 'Moon Man' and talk to them and 'how do you do' them, and that's what they want and it's fun for us," he said. "I'm at the same level with the kids. You have an ex-ballplayer who's immature, who gets along with kids. I have a ball doing these things."

Minton has since moved back to Arizona. According to the *Arizona Republic,* he coached youngsters at Extra Innings, an indoor baseball and software training facil-itiy in Tempe, Ariz. until it closed in June 2011.

BOB BRENLY

DIAMONDBACK IN THE ROUGH

Bob Brenly was having a rough week—and things were about to get worse. His 2004 Arizona Diamondbacks were struggling with a 14-20 record and were mired in last place, eight-and-a-half games behind the division-leading Dodgers. It's only May 14, but the local media were already speculating his managerial job was in jeopardy. Ace Randy Johnson made matters worse, first by publicly second-guessing Brenly for pulling him from a 1-1 game in the seventh inning, a game the D-Backs later lost. Then the day before, the southpaw flamethrower dissed the team after pitching brilliantly for the second time in a week, but still losing 1-0.

"It's a lot of money to come out to a ballgame and lately, it's probably better spent going to the movies than coming to watch the Diamondbacks," Johnson told reporters.

Brenly, the Diamondbacks' manager since 2001, walked into his office at Bank One Ballpark that day, knowing he'd face a firestorm of questions after Johnson bad-mouthed the team in the morning papers. Four hours before a Friday game against the Montreal Expos, Brenly is relaxing in his office. Music blares from his stereo. On top of his spacious wooden desk is a mound of neatly stacked paper—pitching and hitting statistics—that he has studied to gear up for the three-game series. His fingers are on his laptop as he surfs the Web to catch up on the latest baseball news.

"I'm reading about 'BK.' He just got sent down to the minors," Brenly says. "BK" is Byung-Hyun Kim, the Diamondbacks' former sidearm closer who was traded away last season to the Boston Red Sox.

"He keeps throwing too much on the side," says Brenly, recalling how he and his coaching staff implored him to save his arm for games and not throw too much between games. The wear-and-tear on Kim's arm has resulted in slower

Bob Brenly became an All-Star catcher in 1984.
© S.F. Giants

velocity on his fastball, about 10 mph slower this year. The Red Sox are dealing with it by sending him down to Triple-A.

"He still hasn't learned," Brenly says, shaking his head.

Brenly—the Giants' 1984 All-Star catcher—spent a lot of time teaching.In 2003 and 2004, a tighter budget and injuries to veterans forced the team to rely on players from Triple-A Tucson. In 2003, the Diamondbacks—filled with rookies nicknamed the "Baby Backs"—finished a respectable 83-79, third place in the National League West. In 2004, the team got even younger with injuries sidelining key players, including first baseman Richie Sexson, second baseman Roberto Alomar, starting pitcher Shane Reynolds, and relievers Matt Mantei and Oscar Villarreal.

Veteran players may make physical errors. They may throw the ball away, for example, but very rarely do they make mental errors, Brenly says. Younger players, however, tend to make both types of mistakes.

"Your patience gets tested on a daily basis," he said. "They try to do too much, trying to make the miraculous play, or trying to throw a guy out when they really have no chance."

As a result, Brenly and his coaching staff spent a lot of time teaching his young players in their first or second seasons in the majors. In fact, Brenly instituted extra fielding practice before games to go over basics, such as fielding bunts and handling rundown plays.

"You have to correct on the fly. Before the game, during the game, after the game, on the plane flights," he said. "Wherever there is a window of opportunity to teach somebody something about the game, we take advantage of it."

Despite the tough start to the season, his players said Brenly kept a positive attitude, an attribute he learned from his mentor Roger Craig, who managed the Giants from 1986 to 1992.

Signed by the Giants as an amateur free agent in 1976, the Ohio University graduate spent five years toiling in the minors before joining the Giants as a 27-year-old rookie near the end of the 1981 season. He spent two years splitting catching duties with Milt May, then won the job in 1984, when he hit .291, with 20 homers and 80 RBIs, and became an All-Star. He was the Giants' starting catcher for four more years, including the 1987 team that won the National League West, his favorite year as a player.

Another highlight was in 1986 when he was an emergency starter at third base and made four errors in one inning to tie a Major League record. He later atoned for the errors by winning the game with his bat. "In the fourth inning, it seemed like every ball got hit to me. I made errors to my forehand and to my backhand. I made a throwing error," he recalled.

Brenly's temper was legendary. After the error-filled inning, teammates fled to one end of the dugout, fully anticipating that he'd break something. "If you were ever going to show a Little League kid how not to act, it would be the Bob Brenly tape," said former Giants outfielder Dan Gladden, now a Twins broadcaster. "He was one of the best at snapping after a bad at-bat. He would come into the dugout, break bats, break helmets and kick equipment."

After his disastrous inning, Brenly surprised his teammates by doing nothing. "This incredible feeling of calm came over me," said Brenly, who then hit a home run to put the Giants on the scoreboard in the fifth, a two-run single to tie the game in the seventh, then a game-winning homer in the ninth.

"Things seemed to go in slow motion. It was almost as if I were watching myself do this," he said. "I remember Roger Craig saying I should be the Comeback Player of the Year for one day."

Craig was a big influence on Brenly, teaching him how to approach the game as a catcher. "It's the nuts and bolts of the ballgame and the strategies involved, and the reasons why you do things," he said.

Brenly, in his late 50s, never planned on managing. After retiring in 1989, Brenly became a Chicago Cubs broadcaster, joining Harry Caray and Thom Brennaman in the radio booth for two years. In 1992, he rejoined the Giants as bullpen coach under Craig, then served three more years on Dusty Baker's coaching staff. Before the 1996 season, Brenly took a job at Fox to become a color commentator. He went on to announce All-Star games, playoff games, and the World Series for Fox's national telecasts. He also became Brennaman's partner in the TV booth when the expansion D-Backs began playing in 1998.

"He's everything you want in a television analyst: He's smart. He knows the game. He's got a great sense of timing, and without a doubt, one of the funniest people in the world today," Brennaman said.

After the D-Backs underachieved during the 2000 season, owner Jerry Colangelo fired manager Buck Showalter. Veteran players had complained loudly about Showalter's strict rules, from bans on earrings and beards to not speaking to the competition before the game. Colangelo needed someone to lighten up the clubhouse and turned to Brenly.

It was an offer Brenly couldn't refuse.

"I played the game because I loved to play it. I coached the game because it was an opportunity to stay close to the Giants, and then the broadcasting thing came up. It was a career I enjoyed, and I could see myself doing that forever," he recalled. "When this opportunity came up, it was just too good to turn down. It was a team that was built to win and win right now."

His first act as manager was to tell the team they could relax. In his first meeting with the team, he showed Showalter's rule book, dropped it on a table with a loud thud, then pulled out a cocktail napkin out of his pocket and read off his rules to the team: "Be on time, play hard and try to win."

The players responded to Brenly's more casual style. In his rookie season as manager, Brenly guided the team to a thrilling World Series victory, beating the Yankees in an improbable come-from-behind Game 7 victory with two outs in the ninth inning.

"Every move he made worked for him that year. He knew the personnel. He just fit right in," said Luis Gonzalez, who blooped the Series-winning hit. "After games, we'd all sit around and have cold beers and talk about the game anyway, so the only difference is he's the manager, not the broadcaster."

Brenly barely remembers the on-field celebration after the World Series. "I looked back at the video after the game and saw myself jumping up and down, running around and hugging and kissing the guys," he said. "I don't remember doing any of it. It was pure emotion bubbling over the top."

❖ ❖ ❖ ❖ ❖ ❖

Life was a bit less jovial that day at Bank One Ballpark. Three hours before the game against the Expos, Brenly was sitting on the dugout bench for his pre-game briefing with reporters. He's surrounded by journalists with a row of television cameras inches from his face. The journalists fired away, asking Brenly about Johnson's diatribe against the team in that day's papers.

"Randy is just frustrated just like everybody else. We expect a lot out of ourselves. I know our fans expect a lot out of us. Randy expects a lot out of himself. And when things don't go the way you hope, it's easy to get frustrated," Brenly said. "And he just vocalized some of those frustrations. I'm sure you could catch any one of us at any given moment, and we may have said something like that… It has no bearing on the ballgame tonight."

The TV crews got the soundbite they needed and scampered off. The remaining journalists peppered Brenly with questions about the series against Montreal. When the questioning was done, Brenly raced out of the dugout to watch batting practice.

Later in the dugout, Gonzalez was waxing his bat as he got ready for practice. Up to that point, all the media speculation on Brenly's job hadn't affected his ability to manage, he said.

"It hasn't shown in the clubhouse," said Gonzalez, who then defended Brenly as manager. "He's awesome. He's played the game, and knows the ups and downs of the game. I enjoy having him as the manager because he's so easy going. He's just a lot of fun, a player-type manager. He's filled with emotion when we don't play well, but that's to be expected. He runs the ship."

Gonzalez dismissed the talk that Brenly's job was in danger. "That will always be written when teams don't play well, but you know what? Very few guys win a World Series as a rookie manager, so when you set the bar high, expectations are high. We will get back to that level."

Brenly was diplomatic and didn't make excuses when asked if Diamondbacks fans have unreasonably high expectations because the seven-year-old franchise had contended nearly every year.

"I think winning the World Series in 2001 and going to the postseason in

2002, the fans have come to expect it. They're greedy, which is good," he said. "The bar is set pretty high, and the expectations are high. When we don't play up to those expectations, they let us know about it. Nobody can expect more out of us than we expect of ourselves."

Brenly expected a lot of out of himself—as a player and as a manager. His solid work ethic—and desire to learn the game of baseball during his playing days—is what made him a good skipper, said Dusty Baker, then the manager of the Chicago Cubs.

"He listens and learns. He learned a lot being under Roger Craig and Frank Robinson, and guys like Mike Krukow, Chili Davis, Jeff Leonard. They were all there about the same time and kind of taught each other," said Baker, a teammate of Brenly's in 1984. "Plus, the fact that he was a good player, but not a great player, and had to work for everything he got. He wasn't a high-round draft choice. He wasn't really even expected to be in the majors. 'BB' understands all facets of the game. He has a strong desire to win."

Just like Craig, Brenly liked to play hunches. Before games, he looked over the statistics: the righty-lefty matchups, the historical matchups between pitchers and hitters, who's hot and who's not. But during a game, he made decisions based on his gut feeling, not on statistics.

"We do all the homework, but once you get out on the field, I believe you have to trust your eyes and your instincts," he said. "A lot of this game is just feelings. What feels right. What doesn't feel right. The numbers are a nice background to have, but you can't go strictly by the numbers."

He certainly did that during the 2001 World Series. Before Game 7, he benched right fielder Reggie Sanders because he felt Danny Bautista would better handle Roger Clemens' high fastball. He also benched first baseman Erubiel Durazo for veteran Mark Grace. "The decision at first base came down to the fact that Mark Grace had played 16 years in the big leagues and deserved to start Game 7," he said. "We just felt that if there were any intangibles to be had, we needed Mark Grace in the game."

Brenly's hunches paid off. Bautista hit a double that drove in the Diamondbacks' first run in the sixth inning. Down 2-1, Grace led off the 9th with a single to start the Diamondbacks' comeback.

For managers, it's easy to manage by the book to avoid getting second-guessed by the media. Brenly was willing to make tough decisions, Baker said. "He's not afraid to be wrong. He's not afraid to try anything."

❖❖❖❖❖❖❖

Brenly was feeling optimistic at the start of the weekend series against the Expos. Richie Sexson, whom the Diamondbacks acquired by trading six players to Milwaukee, was about to come off the disabled list. Pitcher Casey Fossum, acquired from Boston for Curt Schilling in the off-season, just came off the disabled list to start that evening's game.

The D-Backs lost the series' opener, 4-3. Arizona took an early 2-0 lead, then battled back to tie the game, 3-3, only to give up the winning run in the ninth. After the game, Brenly walked into the media conference room with a frown on his face. It was a game the D-Backs could have won. Nevertheless, Brenly said kind words about Montreal starter Tomo Okha, then praised Fossum, who tossed five innings and gave up three runs on five hits.

"For his first time out, all things considered, he did a pretty good job at keeping us in the ballgame," he said. "His stuff was good."

But the teacher in Brenly also came out. Two Expos stole bases off Fossum.

"We will work on speeding up his delivery a little bit. This is a team that will take advantage of guys who are slow to the plate, and they try to do that every chance they get," Brenly said. "That's something that we will work on the side. But overall, he did a nice job."

That weekend, the Diamondbacks were swept by the Expos, the worst team in baseball. Colangelo, the owner, felt compelled to give Brenly—in the final year of his contract—a vote of confidence. Colangelo blamed the players, noting that Mantei had blown three games as a closer early in the season. The print media speculated that the vote of confidence means Brenly will at least survive the upcoming 13-game road trip.

When the Diamondbacks got shut out in the second game of the Expos series, however, the eternal optimism Brenly learned from Craig took a backseat as he lashed out at his team.

"We suck. That's what it is. I mean, when we need to pitch well, we don't pitch well. When we need to hit well, we don't hit well. When we need to catch the ball, we don't catch the ball. We are equal opportunity [expletive]," Brenly told reporters. "That's the only way you can put it. We find ways to lose games, and I'm real [expletive] tired of it."

Opposing managers were sympathetic to Brenly's plight. Players get the credit for winning, but the manager gets the blame for losing, said then-Giants skipper Felipe Alou.

"That is the way it is, has always been," Alou said. "Teams that have won, you don't usually hear the name of the manager. They start losing, the manager's name starts to show up after every loss. And then the roof will start to come off, so you have to be tough. Brenly has always been a tough guy."

Brenly is managing a team with high expectations, but the team is in transition, Alou noted. "If you got the horses, you got a heck of a shot at making it," he said. "Once you start losing people on one team and bringing in the young guys, and the old guys get older, it is not easy to maintain a winning situation during a transition type of time."

❊ ❊ ❊ ❊ ❊ ❊ ❊

At the start of a crucial 13-game road trip, on May 18, 2004, Johnson tossed a perfect game. Brenly was in the middle of the mob, embracing Johnson, slapping him on the back. At that moment, a week's worth of angst disappeared. It was the perfect time for a group hug.

Brenly and his coaches talked about bringing in Donnie Sadler as a defensive replacement, but didn't want to make any changes for fear it would break up Johnson's rhythm. He even resorted to superstition.

"My knuckles are sore from banging on Matt Kata's bat. I was standing in front of the bat rack, and his bat happened to be right there by my right hand. And before every pitch from the sixth inning on, I was tapping on that bat," he said in a television interview with Fox Sports Arizona immediately after the game. "I tell you, for a perfect game, and to win a ballgame like this, that's as hard as we've been grinding all year on the bench."

But the perfect game was just a temporary reprieve.

After a 9-20 record in May, Colangelo gave Brenly another vote of confidence, telling the media that Brenly would manage as long as June wasn't as bad as May. The D-Backs ended June with a 10-17 record, including a brutal 11-game losing streak.

Colangelo fired Brenly on July 3, and replaced him with third base coach Al Pedrique. The D-Backs' record stood at 29-50.

"Bob's an old pro. Bob felt it, he read it, he heard it. You know when things are happening," Colangelo said in a press conference.

Brenly wasn't to blame for the team's woes, added Colangelo, who months later was ousted as Diamondbacks CEO by new ownership. The D-Backs, who were expected to contend that season, were devastated by injuries. After coming off the disabled list, Sexson promptly reinjured his shoulder and missed the rest of the year. Kata, who took over for the injured Alomar, dislocated his left shoulder in a dive attempt and needed season-ending surgery. And newly-minted closer Jose Valverde went down with his own shoulder injury. Near the end of Brenly's tenure, ten players on the 25-man roster began the year in Triple-A.

"In no way shape or form is this change a reflection on Bob Brenly, nor are we putting any blame on Bob Brenly for the state of affairs of our baseball team," Colangelo said. "With the number of injuries and bad luck we've had this year, he's a casualty. It's as simple as that."

Players and coaches that day praised Brenly, saying he stayed optimistic until the end. Pitcher Brandon Webb said Brenly held multiple team meetings to try to fire up the players. "I hate to see him going. I really liked him," Webb said. "Usually BB was trying to keep things positive."

Fox Sports immediately announced that it would like to rehire Brenly to broadcast again, but Brenly disappeared from public view the rest of the sum-

While manager of the Diamondbacks, Brenly met Senator John McCain.
Arizona Diamondbacks photo

mer. He gave one interview the day after he was fired and said he believed the team could still turn things around.

"There was still a tiny little part of me that was hopeful as I went to his office that maybe he would put an end to all the speculation with an extension, but obviously the majority of my mind knew that wasn't going to happen," Brenly told MLB.com. "Right up to the minute I got fired... I still thought someway, somehow we could get the kids playing well and at least make the teams at the top of the division sweat a little bit. And I still believe the talent is there. It's young talent and they're going to make mistakes and you're just going to have to be patient with them."

❊ ❊ ❊ ❊ ❊ ❊ ❊

Brenly is a Giant at heart. Years ago, he almost managed the Giants, but it wasn't meant to be.

Without putting it in writing, Giants owner Bob Lurie and general manager Al Rosen groomed Brenly to replace Craig when he retired, said Brennaman,

Brenly's friend and former broadcasting partner.

In 1992, Brenly served as a coach under Craig. But when Lurie sold the team, Peter Magowan's ownership group hired Baker as manager. Brenly went on to coach under Baker for three years before returning to broadcasting.

"It's the story that's never been told," Brennaman said. "All the foundation was laid for Brenly to become the next manager of the Giants."

He got another chance seven years later in Arizona. Brenly grew from his experience as manager of the D-Backs, learning to better motivate and communicate with players, Brennaman said. As a player, Brenly never needed motivation to play hard. But players sometimes need a pat on the back or a chewing out to play well.

"He learned a lot over the four years as manager," Brennaman said. "It's been hard for him at times to understand the makeup of different personalities. Some guys do need motivation. He's grown well into that."

Two months after getting fired, Brenly and his wife celebrated their 30th wedding anniversary in August. They met in kindergarten in their hometown of Coshocton, Ohio. He and his wife began dating in high school and married during college. They have two children: Lacey and Michael.

While the D-Backs went on to lose more than 110 games, Brenly spent the rest of the summer traveling with his son Michael and watching him play baseball across the country, Brennaman said. Michael, a catcher and first baseman, played in an invitation-only summer league for the nation's top high schoolers.

Brenly joined the Chicago Cubs in 2005 as a TV analyst. After eight years in the Windy City, Brenly has returned to the Diamondbacks for the 2013 season, where he handles color commentary.

JOEL YOUNGBLOOD

DOT-COM, DOT-BOMB

In 1999, the economy boomed, e-commerce was the rage, and extravagance was the norm. The American workforce and investors alike were intoxicated by pre-IPO start-ups and stock options. As stock prices soared, tech companies, with seemingly bottomless budgets, threw lavish launch parties with unlimited food and bar tabs, famous rock bands, melting ice sculptures, and even tarot card readers.

Joel Youngblood wanted to join the fun—and that year, he got the chance.

At a Cincinnati Reds fantasy baseball camp in Florida, Youngblood caught the eye of one of the fantasy campers. Charles "Junior" Johnson, chief executive of PurchasePro.com, offered him a job at his start-up, which built technology that allowed companies to conduct business over the Internet. Youngblood, then a Milwaukee Brewers' coach, became employee No. 98.

The former Giant joined PurchasePro as a salesman, but was quickly promoted to advanced project management. Armed with PowerPoint presentations, he explained to prospective clients how procurement over the Web would save them money and give them the best prices for the supplies they need. He was in on the company's initial public offering. The stock price closed at $27 on its first day of trading, reaching $224 at its height.

"It was wonderful to be in a young, growing company. There was excitement, energy," recalled Youngblood, now in his early 60s. "It was a race to get your company out there before other companies could get theirs out."

Like many Internet start-ups, however, the hype didn't match reality. After about four years, as revenue dwindled and losses mounted, the company's stock plummeted to around $1 to $2 a share. After three rounds of layoffs, Youngblood knew the writing was on the wall.

"When my baseball card was worth more than my stock, I knew it was time

Joel Youngblood batted .317 for the Giants in 1983.
© S.F. Giants

to leave," Youngblood joked.

PurchasePro went bankrupt in September 2002, but Youngblood doesn't have regrets. He enjoyed the experience, and the fast-paced, competitive atmosphere as his company battled other start-ups, such as Ariba and CommerceOne, for a piece of the emerging e-business software market.

He enjoyed teaching the benefits of PurchasePro's technology to prospective clients, such as management of large hotel chains. The parties for the Las Vegas-based company were great, too, featuring bands like Earth, Wind and Fire and K.C. and the Sunshine Band.

"You thought it would never end," said Youngblood.

Youngblood, who lives in Arizona with his wife Beckie, began his 14-year playing career in 1976 as a utility player for the Big Red Machine. He played all defensive positions, including catcher, as Cincinnati captured the World Series title that year. He became a full-time starter in 1979 for the New York Mets, batting .275, with 16 home runs and 60 RBIs.

Youngblood, a Houston native, was a Mets All-Star in 1981, and later signed as a free agent with the Giants, where he played the infield and outfield from 1983 to 1988. His best season with San Francisco was his first, when he hit a career-high 17 homers with 53 RBIs and led the team with a .292 batting average.

He frequently talked about hitting in the clubhouse, and was always trying to find some edge or technique to improve his stroke, teammates said. Hitting was hard, but Youngblood learned to simplify it, said former Giants third baseman Matt Williams.

"He would refer to this little square box all the time. 'All we have to control is this box. Everything else doesn't matter because the pitcher's going to have to throw the ball into that box. If he doesn't, you take it,'" Williams recalled. "And we all said, 'Blood, it's not that simple.' And he'd say, 'Yes it is!' It worked for him, but it didn't work for the rest of us."

He also enjoyed hunting with teammates Will Clark and Mike LaCoss. "He'd come to the ballpark with his camouflage on, and his bows and arrows, guns and pictures of his deer kills," said former Giants infielder Chris Speier. "He was just a nut."

The three avid hunters, along with Mike Krukow and Jeffrey Leonard, kept the clubhouse loose, Youngblood said. "We used to get on each other in the clubhouse. We yapped it up and kidded around. It was a lot of fun."

Youngblood retired at age 37 after playing his final season with the Reds in 1989. He has many favorite highlights in his-14 year career, in which he batted .265, while smacking 80 home runs and driving in 422 RBIs. Youngblood once went five for five in a game. He's also the only player ever to have two hits for two different teams on the same day.

It was August 4, 1982, and Youngblood began the day in Chicago as a New

Youngblood experienced the dot-com boom and bust.
Photo by Matt Johanson

York Met, where he started the game and hit a two-run RBI single off Ferguson Jenkins. In the third inning, at around 2:30 P.M., he was traded to the Montreal Expos, who were playing in Philadelphia that night.

So he quickly said goodbyes to his teammates, scampered back to the team's Chicago hotel, and caught the next flight to Philadelphia. From the airport, he took a cab to Veterans Stadium, and arrived in the dugout at about 9 P.M., with the game in the third inning. He was sent into the game as a defensive replacement in the sixth inning, then singled off Steve Carlton. He had two hits off two future Hall of Famers for two different teams. He didn't know he was the first major leaguer to accomplish the feat until the media made a big deal about it the next day.

"It was a demanding day," Youngblood said. "The Expos said they were short on players and asked me to try and get there for the game, and it was my mental makeup to do that."

Krukow said Youngblood was a hard-working teammate that everyone could count on. "He was a guy you could always tease. He had a half-goofy laugh that made everyone else laugh," Krukow said. "When the game started, he gave you every ounce he had. He never dogged it. He ran out every ball, played hard and had a great arm. He'd give you a great at-bat."

After retiring, Youngblood coached in the minor leagues for the Baltimore organization for four years. Then he coached in the major leagues for another five years, first in Cincinnati, then in Milwaukee, where he coached third base, the outfield, and base running.

After several years of climbing the corporate ladder, Youngblood is now helping minor leaguers try to climb up to the major leagues. As hitting coach for the Arizona Brewers, he worked on hitting fundamentals but also taught them the mental approach to hitting. After three decades in baseball, Youngblood has a trained eye that can instantly spot mistakes.

"One of my best attributes as a teacher is I didn't hit .300 all the time. I studied the game enough and understand where I failed and why I was successful," he said.

One important attribute he teaches his young hitters is to practice correctly and understand what they're trying to do it at the plate. For example, when he asks players what they're trying to do with the bat, the typical response is, "Hit the ball hard." That's correct, Youngblood says, but hitting is more than that. Batters have to try to hit line drives, not fly balls or grounders.

"Line drives eliminate the amount of time the defense has to get to the ball," he said. "When you practice, practice hitting a line drive."

Youngblood, who has two grown children, doesn't go hunting as much these days. He loves computers, and has three of them networked together in his house. In the future, he plans to take computer science classes, so he can write his own software programs.

One thing he's sure of: he loves teaching. At PurchasePro, he taught people about the benefits of the technology. In baseball, he's teaching hitting.

"There are a lot of opportunities in the world today," he said. "I have been blessed with many opportunities in my life. If I stay in baseball, or take any other adventure, it would be something at home and some type of teaching."

Youngblood joined the Arizona Diamondbacks organization in 2007 and is now in is in his seventh year with the organization. He is currently the team's Minor League outfield and baserunning coordinator.

DAVE DRAVECKY

"How Precious Life Is"

Cancer took away Dave Dravecky's baseball career and his left arm, but it never took away his spirit.

It's been more than 20 years since Dravecky touched Giants fans' hearts with his public battle against cancer, his determination to play again despite doctors' warnings that he would never pitch again—and his stirring comeback in August 1989, when in front of 34,810 adoring fans at Candlestick Park, an emotional, but determined Dravecky tossed eight strong innings to defeat the Cincinnati Reds 4-3.

It was shaping up to become the feel-good story of the year until five days later, when he broke his arm delivering a pitch in Montreal. His pitching arm broke because it was weakened from surgery when doctors cut out half his arm muscle to remove the cancer. For many Giants fans, the horrifying TV replay of Dravecky collapsing on the mound, clutching his arm in pain as first baseman Will Clark and the rest of the infield raced to his aid, is still a vivid memory.

Shortly after, the cancer returned and doctors amputated his left arm and shoulder to get rid of the cancer and save his life. Because of the pain and stress from the illness, Dravecky tumbled into depression. He not only had to cope with the loss of his arm and his dream career, but he had to wrestle with what to do with the rest of his life.

Today, Dravecky is happy again. He devotes his life to giving inspiration to others through motivational speeches, books, and "Dave Dravecky's Outreach of Hope," his non-profit ministry, which provides resources and encouragement to people suffering from cancer, depression, or other serious illnesses. Essentially, the ministry allows Dravecky to help people the same way others helped him.

"With suffering, the greatest need is to provide encouragement," Dravecky said. "Our society has become so immersed in the quick fix, to getting over suf-

Dave Dravecky inspired fans with his comeback game after cancer surgery in 1989.
© S.F. Giants

fering quickly to getting over grieving quickly. Today, when you lose a loved one in other parts of the world, you mourn and dress in black for months. We expect people to get over it in three weeks."

There is no timetable for those who are hurting. They need friends and family on hand to lend emotional support, Dravecky said.

"It breaks our hearts. There are segments of our society that understand, but a large segment of society doesn't get it. There are so many lonely people out there," he added. "It's sad and compels us to do what we do and really say, 'We want to be there for you. We can't be there fiscally, but through encouraging you and sending resources to you, there's someone out there who cares.'"

He and his wife Jan got through their pain through the support from friends, family, and their deep faith in Christianity. In fact, Dravecky remembers how former Giants teammate Atlee Hammaker helped him through one particularly tough period. It was shortly after his baseball career had ended, and Dravecky was traveling alone to Memphis, Tennessee, where he was scheduled to deliver a speech. That day, Hammaker called Jan to check up on Dravecky, and Jan told him that Dravecky wasn't doing well.

"I was in Memphis and didn't want to be there. I was in a deep depression," Dravecky recalled. "He called me up and he said, 'I will be there within the next couple of hours.' For the next three days, he was just there to encourage me."

It's a summer morning, and Dravecky is talking by phone from his office in Colorado Springs, Colorado, where he runs his ministry with Jan. He doesn't draw a salary from the ministry, so to make a living, he gives motivational speeches between about 25 times a year to audiences that vary from students from kindergarten through high school to employees at Fortune 500 companies.

While he takes a break from speech-making during the summer, his ministry and his five-person staff keeps him busy. Outreach of Hope offers Web articles, audiotapes, videotapes, books and his ministry's own *The Encourager Magazine*, which provide guidance, advice and inspiration to people who are suffering. It also gives referrals to churches, Christian counseling organizations, and national cancer organizations, such as the Kids Cancer Network.

Dravecky makes phone calls and writes notes of encouragement to those who request it. Sometimes it's a boy who was recently diagnosed with cancer. Other times, it's an adult who's just gone through surgery. He also spends time reaching out to his supporters who donate money to his ministry. When people write or call the ministry requesting prayers, Dravecky and his staff take the time to pray for them.

"All of us participate in praying," he said. "Sometimes when people say they will pray for you, you wonder if they really do. So after we've prayed, we send a positive note to the individual acknowledging that we prayed for them."

Dravecky, who has since learned to write right-handed, also spends a considerable amount of time signing autographs to those who request it. He signs every

© S.F. Giants

copy of his ten books, available through his ministry. His most popular book, *Comeback*, details his battle with cancer and how his strong faith in Christianity helped him survive the experience. He's also written several books with Jan, including *Stand By Me*, which provides tips for people who want to help friends and family who are hurting.

Dravecky doesn't devote all his time to work, however. With his summer vacation just starting, Dravecky looks forward to relaxing and spending time on the golf course. In fact, he had just seen a TV commercial for a fairway wood golf club and is considering a new one to help him with his game. While Dravecky is an amputee, it hasn't stopped him from pursuing his love of sports. He also skis in the winter and hunts with one arm.

"I've had so many challenges as an amputee that I try to do everything I can," he explained.

He even returned to the baseball diamond, having sponsored independent baseball teams who compete in summer tournaments across the country,. Dravecky acted like a roving instructor, helping coaches with the pitching staff. The teams, which played under the moniker, "Dave Dravecky Baseball Gamers," were heavily influenced by the Giants: their uniforms were orange and black. Their black caps had an orange "G" in front, similar to the Giants' Spring Training caps.

Dravecky's goal was to help children pursue their baseball dreams , but in the process, also build their character and help them become better people. Some of the principles the coaches taught included: be humble; Have courage; Always work hard; Don't be afraid of failure; and Respect your parents. "Baseball is in my blood," he said. "It's been a lot of fun developing kids' baseball skills and helping them build character."

As a baseball player, Dravecky had a lot of character, and his teammates respected him for it.

"Obviously, he's as good a Christian and a human being as there has ever been on the face of the earth, but when you gave him the ball, and sent him to the mound, he wasn't afraid to knock an opponent to the ground," said Bob Brenly, a catcher for the Giants in the '80s and teammate of Dravecky's. "He was just a tremendous competitor and seemed to have his priorities in order."

Chris Speier, an infielder for the Giants in the 1970s and 1980s, said Dravecky's passion and infectious enthusiasm for the game energized his teammates. His teammates awarded him the Willie Mac Award as the most inspirational Giant in 1989.

"He was the most inspirational man I ever played with. He never gave up, he never gave in," Speier said.

Dravecky has fond memories of San Francisco. A 21st round draft pick, Dravecky toiled four years in the minors before making his Major League debut in 1982 as a 26-year-old rookie, helping the Padres reach the World Series in 1984 as a reliever and spot-starter.

Midway through the 1987 season, with the Giants needing to shore up its starting pitching, Dravecky was traded to San Francisco, along with reliever Craig Lefferts and third baseman Kevin Mitchell, in a blockbuster deal that sent third baseman Chris Brown and pitchers Mark Davis, Keith Comstock, and Mark Grant to San Diego. Giants fans instantly warmed up to Dravecky, who led the Giants to the playoffs with a 7-5 record and pitched brilliantly in two starts in the National League Championship Series against the St. Louis Cardinals.

"I was really not knowing what to expect, but I knew I was coming to an organization with a great tradition," Dravecky recalled. "We met with [manager] Roger Craig, [pitching coach] Norm Sherry, and [general manager] Al Rosen. They invited us to the coaches' office and told us, 'You are the key to us getting into the playoffs.' That meeting set the stage for what became a love affair with San Francisco."

In the NLCS, after the Giants dropped Game 1, Dravecky tossed a complete game, two-hit shutout in front of 55,000 rabid Cardinals fans at Busch Stadium as the Giants evened the series with a 5-0 win against Cardinals ace John Tudor. In Game 6, with the Giants leading the series 3-2 and needing one win to reach the World Series, Dravecky gave a strong pitching performance, giving up only one run in six innings. But the Giants' bats fell silent—as San Francisco lost that game in a heartbreaker, 1-0 loss. They would lose the series a day later.

Dravecky had first noticed a lump on his left arm before the playoffs began. Neither he nor the team doctors were overly concerned because it didn't affect his pitching. But the lump grew bigger during the off-season.

An initial test in January 1998 showed that the lump was not serious. Dravecky pitched Opening Day that April, tossing a three-hitter in a 5-1 win. He went on to start seven more games before going on the disabled list with arm pain. Dravecky discovered the tumor was cancerous when detailed tests were performed in September. Weeks later, doctors removed the cancer, and half his deltoid muscle in his arm, during an eight-hour surgery.

Dravecky was determined to pitch again. He spent the next ten months doing strenuous workouts to rehabilitate his arm. After a few starts in the minor leagues during the summer of 1989, the Giants—in the midst of another heated pennant race—brought Dravecky back up to the big league team.

His courageous comeback captivated not only San Francisco, but the entire nation. The nearly 35,000 fans in attendance at Candlestick Park showered Dravecky with standing ovations even before the game began—when he threw in the bullpen during his pre-game warmups and when his name was announced. He received another standing ovation after a perfect 1-2-3 first inning, and another when he was replaced by closer Steve Bedrosian in the ninth inning.

Dravecky threw eight strong innings of four-hit ball that day, earning a 4-3 victory. Dravecky said the game and the outpouring of support from fans were overwhelming and the highlight of his career.

"It was incredible. It was an amazing memory forever etched in my heart, simply because of the circumstances of my situation. That outside of a miracle, I would never pitch again," Dravecky recalled. "It was very special. Obviously, I realized how precious the game of baseball was, and how precious life is, and how being able to experience that moment, all that surrounded it, was amazing."

For Dravecky, that day was also special because he helped raise nearly $200,000 to help Alex Vlahos, a six-year-old San Mateo leukemia patient, in his efforts to find a bone marrow donor. Giants radio station KNBR, for example, donated money to Vlahos for every pitch Dravecky threw.

"Not only did I come back and play, I saw a community rise up and help a person they didn't know," he said.

But in his next start in Montreal, his valiant comeback and his career ended as he broke his arm pitching to Tim Raines in the sixth inning. While on the mend that summer, Dravecky broke his left arm again during the on-field celebration moments after the Giants won the National League pennant. That fall, the cancer returned, and Dravecky announced his retirement from baseball. When radiation treatments did no good, doctors amputated his left arm and shoulder to save his life.

He won the last game he ever pitched and ended his eight-year career with a 64-57 record and a 3.13 ERA. He didn't know it at the time, but his fight with cancer served as a bridge to his next career, and the creation of his ministry in 1991.

When his arm snapped in Montreal, Dravecky remembers thinking that something bigger was going on. "Baseball was just a stepping stone to something more important, and it culminated with that day," he said. "I didn't know what that meant at the time. There were struggles to follow, a lot of struggles to follow before I got to the place where I saw where the bigger picture was. That was a significant moment that set the stage to what I'm doing today."

Looking back, at the height of his baseball career, Dravecky lost sight of what was important to him. His struggle with cancer helped set him straight, he said.

"There were times when, quite frankly, it was all about me. Life revolved around me. That was a selfish thing," he said. "Sometimes we can get caught up in life and be distracted by what we think is important until tragedy hits. It's a wakeup call. A phrase I use when I speak is, 'It's not what you do that matters most, it's who you are.' Cancer helped me put that in perspective."

When he was diagnosed with cancer, he realized his relationships were what mattered most, not what he did for a career, he said. "My life is about my relationship with God, my relationship with my wife, kids, friends, and associates."

Dravecky is a different kind of role model these days. In baseball, he took seriously the way he played the game because he knew tens of thousands of people were watching, especially kids. But baseball was entertainment. Now he deals with life and death situations.

"With baseball, we made people happy or sad, based on whether we won or lost that day," he said. "Now I'm dealing with people who hurt. I've stepped onto a playing field that's sacred because it's someone else's pain and suffering. We have the privilege of encouraging hundreds of people every year through our resources. Baseball doesn't come close to that."

The ministry was originally called the Dave Dravecky Foundation. Dravecky renamed Outreach of Hope to better reflect its goals. Christianity is an important part of Dravecky's message.

Dravecky inspires others through his speeches, books and ministry.
Dave Dravecky's Outreach of Hope photo

"The experiences I had in my life helped me come face to face with my own mortality, and the reality of when that happens in our life, we are compelled to think about what happens after life," he said. "Because of my journey spiritually and my decision 20-plus years ago to follow Jesus Christ and become a Christian has given me hope in knowing that because of that faith, I will live forever, and that's what I embrace everyday. And what compels me to want to be a source of encouragement for others."

Dravecky will possibly write another book, this time on his thoughts on baseball and the way it should be played. It will be aimed at youngsters and the coaches who coach them.

"I am very content, really having a deep inner joy of where I'm at," he said. "I want to continue to be the man God wants me to be, the best husband, the best father and best friend I can be. And in the context of what I'm doing, to keep in mind that life really isn't always about me."

San Francisco helped him understand that in 1989, when it reached out to help young Vlahos, who was fighting for his life, Dravecky said. Vlahos died the next spring, in 1990, after two unsuccessful bone marrow transplants. Dravecky will always have a soft spot for San Francisco's baseball fans because of their outpouring of support for Vlahos.

"It's a very special place for us because of the people," he said. "I would hope that they would remember how much I loved God and how much I loved my family, and how much I loved baseball in San Francisco," he said. "Those are the things that really mattered to me, and to this day are very important to me."

Dravecky still runs his non-profit ministry, now called Endurance with Jan and Dave Dravecky. In late 2012, the couple moved from Colorado to Turlock, Calif. He continues to do motivational speaking, and for the past two years, he's worked for the Giants' marketing department as a special assistant at large. Part of his duties is meeting with corporate sponsors in their suites at AT&T Park. "I've enjoyed it thoroughly. It's been a wonderful experience," he says.

CHRIS SPEIER

"JACK OF ALL TRADES"

Fast approaching his 500th home run, Ken Griffey Jr. stepped to the plate in the seventh inning of a 2004 interleague contest between the visiting Reds and the Athletics. Oakland's offense had jumped on Cincinnati for ten runs, but starting pitcher Barry Zito had surrendered five to the Reds when Griffey came to bat with two outs and a runner on first.

Junior shot a ground ball hard up the middle that would usually be an easy base hit. But the Oakland infield employed a defense that Giants fans know well, a shift far to the right designed to take hits away from left-handed batters who pull the ball. Shortstop Bobby Crosby fielded the ball behind second base and retired Griffey to end the scoring threat. In the Oakland dugout, bench coach Chris Speier clapped his hands and smiled.

Researching the decisions that help win ballgames was a big part of Speier's job. Speier created spray charts that show where opposing batters hit every fair ball against A's pitchers. He also prepared a batting average report of every opposing hitter vs. Oakland's pitchers, and Athletics hitters against the opponents' pitchers. The team used the information to determine its lineup, to position its defense, to decide how to pitch opposing hitters, and to determine pitching changes.

"Sometimes you get it right, and sometimes you don't, but it's a game of percentages," Speier said. "You could do all the right things, and the batter could still get a hit, and it may be the complete opposite of where you were playing him. But if you keep doing it enough, the percentages are probably going to show his tendencies. Unless he's changed, and then you've got to rethink it again."

Speier additionally reviewed the advance scouting reports and collected input from Oakland's players who have faced upcoming opponents.

All-Star shortstop Chris Speier led the
National League in fielding percentage in 1975.
© S.F. Giants

"It seems like a lot of homework for a three-game series," Speier said. "But the more you prepare, the more information you have available to you, the better chance you have of gaining an advantage. It's better than flipping a coin."

✷ ✷ ✷ ✷ ✷ ✷

Preparation and hard work were staples of Speier's playing career, too, which he proved at his first Giants Spring Training camp in 1970. Speier, 19, showed up ten days before the rookies were due, a move which paid a handsome reward.

"I was fortunate that I got a chance to work out with the Double-A club," Speier said. "When the coaches had their big pow-wow at the end of Spring Training for slotting all the players, the Double-A manager stood up for me and said he wanted to take me. I skipped two levels of ball by showing up early.

"That was an ethic instilled in a very young age with me. To work hard was just part of the job," he said. "To be honest, I had such a fear of failure that I would do all the physical things that I needed to do so I knew that I was at least prepared."

Failure did not sit well with the young shortstop. Giants pitcher Jim Barr, another Minor League prospect at the time, recalled a very different Speier than the calm, collective coach in the A's dugout. "He was already a good shortstop back then, but he had a temper when he first came up," Barr said. "If he didn't get a hit, he would fire that bat and helmet with the best of them."

Speier agreed he was hotheaded. "I took my failures really, really hard in the beginning," he said. "I was very demonstrative about failing or making outs or making errors and losing. And it carried over. I think as I matured I learned that this is a game of failure. You have 162 games, and not every one of them is the seventh game of the World Series. I grew up a little bit."

The religious conviction Speier gained during his career was part of that change, he said.

"I gained an understanding and a belief that there are a lot of things much more important than this game of baseball," Speier said. "I believe that God had given me a gift of being able to play this game, and what I wanted to do was be the best player I possibly could under the circumstances as my gift back to Him. I think it definitely had something to do with quieting things down."

After only one year in the minors, Speier joined the Giants as the starting shortstop in 1971.

"I saw Mays and McCovey in the field, and Juan Marichal on the mound," Speier said. "I said, 'What am I doing here?' It was a great feeling."

The Giants won the National League West that year, but struggled long afterwards as the front office dumped salary and its star players. The team stopped winning, and attendance at Candlestick plummeted.

"We went into a tailspin. It wasn't fun," Speier said. "We all hoped things would turn around. It took a lot longer to turn around than I was there."

Individually, Speier improved his offensive game, hitting .269 and clubbing 15 homers in 1972, when he represented the Giants in the first of three consecutive All-Star Games. In that era, shortstops made their greatest contributions on defense, and Speier excelled at that, leading the National League in 1975 with a fielding percentage of .982.

"He was a very determined player, and he never was afraid to make an error," said second baseman Tito Fuentes.

The Giants traded Speier early in the 1977 campaign to Montreal, where he would play for eight seasons. Stints in St. Louis, Minnesota, and Chicago followed.

Before the 1987 season, the Giants signed him again, this time as a utility player, "which I loved," Speier said. "It was very challenging."

The former teammate of Mays, McCovey, and Marichal joined a whole new cast of Giants stars like Will Clark, Matt Williams, and Robby Thompson. Speier divided his time between shortstop, second base, and third base during his last three seasons as the Giants took the division twice and won the pennant in 1989. Speier retired in 1989 with a lifetime .249 batting average, .971 fielding percentage, and 19 seasons in the major leagues.

❁ ❁ ❁ ❁ ❁ ❁ ❁

Speier turned in a totally new direction following his departure from baseball, helping to create a school in Scottsdale, Arizona that four of his six children would attend. Speier worked at the Ville De Marie Academy for about three years as principal, physical education coach, substitute teacher and even janitor. A private school with a Catholic curriculum, Ville De Marie began with 40 students from kindergarten through tenth grade.

"A number of families weren't really happy with [public] education," Speier said. "I was the only one who could devote that kind of time to it and not take a salary."

Latin and theology are among the school's required subjects. Students attend mass and confession regularly. There seems little overlap between the baseball world and the pious, academic setting Speier and the other founders created, except perhaps for the uniforms both players and students are required to wear. Yet Speier embraced the challenge of filling what he and other parents saw as a void in the educational spectrum.

"We had no buildings, no books, no teachers, no equipment, nothing. We started from scratch," Speier said. "It was quite an accomplishment and a lot of fun going through it. I thought it was very enjoyable to be involved with young kids, see their development, and be a part of that."

As the student population doubled and the academy expanded to a K-12 school, Speier decided to step aside.

Speier hits ground balls during the Athletics' infield practice.
Photo by Matt Johanson

"I didn't have any educational background in regards to teaching," he said. "I only had one year of college, to play baseball. They needed somebody else to take it to that next level, and I was getting itchy to get back into baseball."

Speier coached for the Chicago Cubs' Double-A affiliate in Orlando, Florida in 1995, and then began four years as a Minor League manager. He compiled a 256-240 record in the Arizona Diamondbacks farm system, from the Pioneer Rookie League to Triple-A in Tucson. Speier returned to the

Major League level when the Milwaukee Brewers hired him as third base coach in 2000.

As third base coach of the Diamondbacks in 2001, Speier won a World Series championship ring. "We had those two horses [pitchers Randy Johnson and Curt Schilling] going out there two times a week. That was just huge," he said. "And we didn't seem to have the big major injuries that decimate clubs and take them out of contention."

Diamondbacks manager Bob Brenly took advantage of Speier's long experience in the infield and made positioning the defense his responsibility. To do that, coaches like Speier consider the opposing hitters' spray charts and the attributes of their starting pitchers.

"Say you have a guy like Randy Johnson, a big, left-handed, hard thrower, and there are a lot of right-handed hitters in the lineup," Speier said. "Because of his slider, a lot of ground balls would go in that hole [between third and short], so we'd move our shortstop a little bit more than their tendencies may have shown."

The pitchers themselves contribute to the decision, especially ones like Schilling, who always has a plan for pitching opponents and corresponding defensive positions, Speier said. "We always left it up to the pitcher," he said. "We'd say, 'If you want us to move a guy, we will, because this is your ball game, and you're pitching out there.'"

Speier took two years off from baseball after the 2001 World Series, but returned in 2004 to fill the position Oakland bench coach Terry Francona vacated to become manager of the Boston Red Sox.

"I was going crazy," Speier said of his layoff. "There wasn't anything outside of baseball that I really enjoyed, that I could see myself doing."

❀❀❀❀❀❀❀

There's a corner spot in each dugout at the Oakland Coliseum that's obscured from the opposing dugout's view. Speier could be spotted there flashing signs to the catcher to thwart the opponent's running game. The catcher relays signs to the pitcher for pitchouts and throws to first to keep base runners close to the bag.

"We'd always like to have our pitchers throw from 1.1 to 1.5 seconds to the plate," Speier said. "Not everybody can do that, but for the most part, everybody's done a good job. They understand that I may have them throw over to first more than they're accustomed to, but I take that opportunity to try to slow these guys down."

The Reds had 41 base runners in the three-game series against Oakland, but didn't steal a single base or even attempt a steal. Cincinnati entered the series with the best record in the National League, but the Athletics swept the series and outscored the Reds, 40-16.

"They hit more balls at our guys than we hit at their guys," Speier laughed. But of course there's more to it than that; Speier's position existed for that reason. The charts and statistics that Speier and other coaches use to formulate game strategy have changed the game. They didn't exist when Speier broke into the majors as a player.

"You can still use intuition," Speier said, "but don't be wrong."

Speier's job also involved working with the infielders during practice, filling in at first and third base, and meeting any other needs that arise.

"When you're a bench coach, you're a jack of all trades," said former Athletics manager Ken Macha, a former Oakland bench coach himself. For example, Macha asked Speier to counsel rookie shortstop Crosby, whose struggles in his first six weeks culminated with a costly dropped pop-up that cost Oakland a game against the Minnesota Twins.

"Take him out to lunch. I want you to talk to him and tell him how it was when you were a rookie, and all the things you've been through," Macha told Speier. After their meeting, Crosby responded with a strong road trip capped by a three-hit performance against Kansas City, including a single, double, home run, and a stolen base. The Athletics swept the Royals series. "I thought Chris was very helpful," Macha said. "You can be called on to do anything, like I was."

Speier later took similar roles with the Chicago Cubs and Cincinnati Reds and hopes to manage one day.

"That's definitely why I got back in. That's a direction I'd like to go," said Speier, though he recognizes the position has drawbacks. "When they show the shots in the dugouts, you see the managers and you never see any of them smiling. It's a very stressful job. But I think I'd like to step into that fire."

MIKE KRUKOW
AND
DUANE KUIPER

GRABBING SOME PINE
WITH KRUK AND KUIP

M ike Krukow and Duane Kuiper—affectionately known as "Kruk" and "Kuip"—have shared the broadcast booth for more than a decade, becoming more popular as Giants announcers than they were as San Francisco players. Krukow was a starting pitcher for seven years, going 20-9 with a 3.05 ERA in 1986. Kuiper was a second baseman and pinch hitter for four seasons.

In the booth, Kuiper speaks with a low-key, relaxed style, but cranks his voice up a notch when drama erupts. Most of Barry Bonds' home run exploits feature Kuiper's signature home run call. As color commentator, Krukow gives fans insightful analysis with comedic flair. Together, the pair brings humor to the broadcasts, often poking fun at the "ball dudes" behind the base lines and unsuspecting fans in the stands. In an interview conducted before the first iteration of this book, Krukow and Kuiper discussed the state of baseball, their broadcasting careers, and their future plans.

Q: What's kept the two of you with the Giants for so many years?
Kuiper: I have no desire to go anyplace else, and the Giants have been kind enough to keep signing me to three- to four-year contracts. I'm a Giant now and that's how it is.

Krukow: I think we were both lucky because we both had radio shows as players and got the Bay Area used to our voices and our perspectives. And then

Duane Kuiper's one career home run is the subject of frequent jokes on the air.
© S.F. Giants

the opportunity just presented itself to talk baseball once we retired. You play here long enough and you understand these are sophisticated fans. They've been educated by Hall of Famers Russ Hodges and Lon Simmons, and Hank Greenwald, who should be a Hall of Famer. We could talk baseball to people who understand what we were talking about. Other broadcasters will get more personal histories. You will get more data and more facts. More statistics. But with us, we pretty much talk about what happens that night in that particular game. And I think this fan base has found that interesting. They've put up with us so far and we hope they keep hanging in there.

Q: How do you keep your enthusiasm high after so many years and so many thousands of games?

Krukow: It's baseball man, c'mon! It's the second best job there is. The only thing better than what we do is playing it. And if you have a hard time coming to the yard doing what we do, something's wrong. This is a wonderful job.

Kuiper: It's because you love the game. The situation and the person who makes the play or hits the home run dictate how enthusiastic you get. It's likely that I'll probably be more excited if Bonds hits a home run than if Scott Rolen does. But on the other hand, I would never shortchange Scott Rolen. I would make a visiting player's home run call exciting enough so that Scott Rolen doesn't get shortchanged.

Q: How do you prepare for games?

Kuiper: Announcers prepare in different ways. I read three sports pages today. So we make sure we cover everything on the local front and things on the national front. Before we go on the air, we will check the Internet. We go to ESPN or CBS for stuff we missed. And if you do games day in and day out, you probably only have to study for one team and that's the visiting team, because the other team you see every day.

Q: So you don't pore through the stats?

Kuiper: I'm not a stats guy. There are situations that come up that warrant a good stat now and then. I don't think people at home care about stats that much unless Bonds is sitting on 699 home runs.

Krukow: Our preparation comes during batting practice. We know our team. We know what type of pitchers they are and the type of swings our hitters have. If someone comes into the league that we don't know, then we watch him during batting practice. We watch him take at-bats, and generally speaking, after three or four at-bats, we pretty much know what type of hitter he is, what side of the plate he looks for in certain fastball counts. So that's how we prepare for it.

Pitcher Mike Krukow saw the Giants rebound from a 100-loss season to the World Series.
© S.F. Giants

Q: Do you have to memorize or write the information down?

Krukow: We just know. Kuip had played in the big leagues for 10 years and I played 13. We prep ourselves the same way now that we prepped as players. We prepare by watching batting practice, and watching guys take groundballs during infield practice, and watching guys throw from the outfield and see what kind of arms they have. And we take that knowledge into the ballgame.

Q: Does any part of the job wear you down, like the travel?

Krukow: Yeah, it does. Some of it is terribly cumbersome. It's hard on the families.

Kuiper: With the travel, we just understand it and accept it. We don't always like it. I suppose in the midst of the 14-day road trip we had, where every hotel you check into at 2:30 or 3 in the morning, yeah, that does get old. But you just make sure you stack up the hours of sleep at another point in the day before you get to the ballpark. If you can get eight hours, you should be ready to go. Take a nap on the plane. Do whatever you can, but just make sure you get as much sleep as you can.

Q: Duane, we know your family lives in the East Bay, but Mike, how often do you get to see your family in San Luis Obispo during the season?

Krukow: April and May are difficult months for me. But right around June, the kids get out of school and join me here. And September is a tough month for me. They go back to school. For a good chunk of summer, we're all together. You make up for it in the off season, when you are with them 100 percent of the day. There are some things you miss, but there are some things you get to see that other guys don't get to see, so it all evens out.

Q: What are your favorite moments as a broadcaster?

Kuiper: Anything in the late innings. Anything with the game on the line. Anything with the Giants on top. Anytime the Giants would clinch a division title, or if they clinch the Wild Card, or move on from one series to the next in the postseason. Those are the moments that you just don't forget.

Krukow: The greatest moment for any broadcaster or fan is when some guy does something he's not supposed to do to win the ballgame. When a bench player comes up and doesn't have much power, and he hits the ball out of the ballpark, like Neifi Perez did in Chicago (in 2004). That won the ballgame and really got the Giants going on a 10-game winning streak. That was really exciting for all of us. It's also exciting to watch with anticipation as Bonds steps up to the batter's box and does what he does. I think the drama of baseball is something that builds slowly. And when it delivers, it's with such completion. It wraps everyone in the ballpark, and everyone gets their nut at the same time. You have 41,000 people going off like that together; it's kind of a special deal.

Q: What is the most significant difference in baseball since you stopped playing?

Krukow: When I played in 1976 to 1990, the umpires allowed you to police the game yourself. If somebody was knocking people down, you had the ability to protect your players. You basically got it resolved and went about your business. Now guys can't do that. Now you retaliate because one or two of your teammates got drilled, and you get kicked out of the ballgame and you're fined and suspended. And when you get into August and September, you can't take key people out of your lineup for four to five games. It's an injustice of the game.

The athletes today are incredibly dedicated. They work 12 months at it. They want to prolong their careers. Obviously, the incentive is financial. But I think the result is they're in great shape. Nutritionally, they take better care of themselves than we did.

Kuiper: Probably that we see more power than we see speed. Speed was such a big part of the game in the 1970s when I played. When we would play the Cardinals, and in every position, they threw guys capable of stealing 25 to 30 bases. We don't see that anymore. We saw Carl Crawford in Tampa Bay and he had 40 steals and we were like, "Whoa!" When I played there were guys all over the place who could steal 40 bases. So I think speed is the one thing that has changed the game a lot.

Q: Is that bad or just the way it is?

Kuiper: I think if you asked fans, "Would you rather see a home run or a stolen base?" they would rather see a home run. Home runs are a big part of the game, and they bring fans to the ballpark.

Q: What are your highlights as Giants players?

Kuiper: It was the last week of the 1982 season, my first year with the Giants. We had a week to go and we were one game out. It was really a mix-and-match bunch of guys. We weren't supposed to win many games at all. We ended up two back, but on the last Friday of the year, we had a chance to go one back, and had we taken two out of three, we would have been tied with the Atlanta Braves. It didn't happen. But for me coming out of Cleveland and not having a chance of winning anything, that week and that whole year were exciting.

*Kuiper's favorite broadcasting moments include
"anything with the Giants on top."*
Photo by Matt Johanson

Krukow: 1987 and 1989 were highlights. Pitching in the playoffs and doing well and winning for the first time as a team was sensational. When you win, there's nothing else like it. When you lose, it's miserable.

Q: So you guys got a bobblehead as broadcasters and not as players. What do you say to that?

Kuiper: It was one of the most fun things that ever happened to us because those are really reserved for the ballplayers. And they put us behind a desk and dropped a microphone in front of us. And our heads bobbled. It was awesome! And so, we got a big kick out of it.

Q: Have you ever thought about coaching or pursuing some other occupation that's close to the game that's not broadcasting?

Krukow: I'm one f-bomb away from being a coach, and that could happen at any given time. If you say something stupid, you get fired. I know that if I ever did piss off the people of San Francisco, I would go back into the game and be a coach someplace. I sure enjoy what I'm doing. I don't want to do anything else.

Q: What would you have done if you didn't go into broadcasting?

Kuiper: I would probably take over my dad's farm in Wisconsin. He still has about 500 acres that was a dairy farm when I was a kid. Now it's corn, soybeans, wheat, barley. I'm not sure if I would have been a good farmer, but I would probably have taken over the farm.

Q: Because you are former Giants, do you find it difficult to make critical comments?

Kuiper: It's easy for me to say, "If you ask J.T. Snow if he should have caught the ball, I'm sure he would tell you he would." That's a lot easier than saying, "Man, I can't believe he didn't catch that ball." So you can be critical. You just have to go about it the right way.

Krukow: Physical errors are just a part of the game. So to overly criticize a person who's made a physical error is weak. However, a mental error that is done repeatedly is one that we will not pull punches with. I just think there's so much negative in this world. If pitchers get lit, there's a guy getting a good at-bat out of it. So why belabor the point that one of your pitchers is getting his ass kicked when you can talk about the guy with the great at-bats? That's the route we choose to take. I never appreciated (criticism) as a player and I don't want to be hypocritical and do something I didn't appreciate as a player.

Q: What else would you not say on the air?

Kuiper: If we see another team tipping off a pitch or doing something that gives the Giants an advantage, we don't say it over the air. We wait until after the game and go into the Giants clubhouse and say, "Hey we see so-and-so tipping a pitch, or that this guy was peeking at the plate." We feel a responsibility. We don't share that with the audience.

Q: How much creative license do you get in your Electronic Arts baseball video game? Do you get to write or supply much of the material you record for the games?

Krukow: We had maybe four two-hour meetings and would sit there and talk about the game and how Duane and I saw things. These guys took all those conversations and put it into the game as best they could. It's been fun. They will give you a script, which looks like a phone book. And you start reading, and when you get into certain things, you say, "I can't say this." They said, "Say what you want to say." So we had free rein. So a lot of what we said was ad-libbed. An enormous amount of hours had gone into it. Now we've worked on it for two years. Just winging it and being creative. (The game designers) listen to us. They listen to every game we do. They will have scripted things we say. It's gotten to the point where we don't have to ad lib as much. We were very well compensated for the experience. When all is said and done, we should have paid them for the right to do it.

Kuiper: It at least put me on the map in my house. My kids never saw me play. And they couldn't care less when I talk about when I played. Being the voice in the video game, all of a sudden, I was a star at least for a little while. My 17 and 14 year old thought that Pops was really cool. For a long time, he wasn't cool, but he is now.

Q: So, the game makers inserted you guys in as players.
Kuiper: Both Mike and I started out at Double-A. My kids didn't even bring me up. I think they brought me to Triple-A.

Krukow: That was kind of a bonus. My kids pulled me out of Norwich, Double-A baseball and I was in the big leagues. They put my number on it, and everything, and they said, "Dad, you are getting your ass kicked. I hope you were better than this guy."

Q: You two are fan favorites among Giants fans. What does that mean to you?
Kuiper: We're fan favorites because we are in thousands of people's homes every night, and we become part of the family. We put people to sleep at times. We wake people up at times. And if you are in an area a long time, you will become part of their family. It's a great Giants family, and I'm just glad to be part of it.

Q: Can you talk about your friendship? Do fans really expect you two to always be together when they see you walking down the street?

"They will have to kick me out the door," says Krukow.
Photo by Matt Johanson

Kuiper: Our friendship is as good a friendship as you are going to get. Fans do think I know where Mike is 24 hours a day, seven days a week. When they see Mike, they feel the same way. I was in Acapulco a couple of years ago, and a guy came up to me and said, "Where's Kruk?" And I went, "I have no idea where Kruk is." And he was stunned because he thought he was probably right around the corner.

Q: How do you want to be remembered as a broadcaster?
Krukow: I hope that people who listen to our broadcast understand how much we love the game and how much fun we have doing this. Because that's one thing we feel about this: it's a game and it's fun.

Q: You both have worked with many announcers with the Giants. What have you learned from Jon Miller, Hank Greenwald, and everyone else?

Krukow: With Hank Greenwald, I learned how to think. I learned how to organize myself to paint word pictures that were concise and accurate, and having done all the radio work I've done made me a better broadcaster in television. Having been around Ted Robinson and Jon Miller, you learn how to relax. You learn that there are certain guidelines that you have to stay within to tell a story correctly. Anyone who's been behind the microphone has always brought a great joy into the game because they love what they do. That's the one thing that we really have here in San Francisco that's a little different.

Kuiper: I learned from each and every one. And everyone I've worked with has been a positive experience. I don't believe there are bad broadcasters. I think there are some broadcasters that people enjoy their styles and some that people don't enjoy their styles.

Q: What will you guys do once you're through with broadcasting?

Kuiper: I will be doing games when I'm half asleep and drooling. Whether that happens at 60 or 80, I will be doing them.

Krukow: I won't walk away. They will have to kick me out of the door. I'm not going anywhere. Kuip and I laugh about this, but we do hope we're doing this when we're 70.

Where Have You Gone?

KEVIN MITCHELL

"O.G."

K evin Mitchell knows the way to Daniel Boone Elementary School well. The retired slugger has visited his 12-year-old daughter's teacher seven times this year, and summer is still three months away. Mitchell has let them both know that if there's any trouble at school, he's siding with the teacher, and he insists on at least 30 minutes of reading for his girl every night.

"I didn't realize how hard it is raising girls, especially as a single parent," Mitchell said. The night before, his daughter and her half-sister, also in Mitchell's care, kept him up so late that he slept through all his morning appointments. Thinking ahead to an upcoming visit to Disneyland and Magic Mountain with the girls and their friends, he sighed and said, "Man, these girls [are] going to drive me crazy."

Mitchell hasn't always acted the part of a model father, though he fathered three daughters with three different women, none of whom he married. He brawled with opponents and teammates during his career. Though he was never convicted, Mitchell has faced charges of rape and battery.

Yet life has changed for the former Giants outfielder and 1989 National League MVP. Mitchell says the jet ski accident that ended his playing days also prepared him for the more important tasks of raising the girls, and working to prevent gang violence in his southeast San Diego neighborhood.

"It's time for me to start giving back," Mitchell says. "I'm on the front line. The Lord has changed my life."

❄ ❄ ❄ ❄ ❄ ❄ ❄

When Mitchell became a Giant in 1987, he had already played for two teams and won a World Series championship ring. Mitchell broke in with the Mets in 1984. Two years later, he played six positions and batted .277 as New York

Kevin Mitchell hit 47 homers and 125 RBIs in 1989.
© S.F. Giants

accomplished an astonishing come-from-behind World Series victory over the Boston Red Sox.

The Mets traded Mitchell to the Padres in 1987, and the Padres dealt him to the Giants on July 4 of the same year. Mitchell played mostly third base for the 1987 National League West champion Giants, batting .306 with 15 home runs and 44 RBIs in the second half of the season.

But his greatest year as a Giant and in the majors arrived in 1989, when he played left field. Mitchell rose to the occasion of batting cleanup, said Dusty Baker, who was then the Giants' hitting coach prior to his 10-year stint as the team's manager.

"Whatever challenges you gave him, it seemed like it made him better," Baker recalled. "And then he went to a big bat, too, a heavier bat. He figured it out. Plus, he'd sit on pitches. He wasn't missing pitches. And he had a heck of an idea what he was looking for and what might be coming."

Mitchell's 47 homers and 125 RBIs powered the Giants to their first pennant since 1962.

"The hard work I did before the season really paid off," said Mitchell. "I hit 12 home runs in Spring Training. And instead of getting weaker late in the season, I was getting stronger." Mitchell credits Baker for helping him fine tune his swing. "I would hit two home runs in a game, and Dusty would say, 'I see something wrong in your swing,' and he'd take me into the cage late at night to work on it," he said.

Mitchell hit .353 with two homers and seven RBIs in the 1989 National League Championship Series against the Chicago Cubs. In retrospect, that was the pinnacle of Mitchell's playing career with the Giants and in baseball.

"It was amazing the power he could generate. It was almost as if at times the game was too easy for him," said Giants broadcaster Hank Greenwald. "There were moments you almost felt that. He had that kind of talent."

During the same year, however, an ex-girlfriend sued Mitchell for allegedly beating her and threatening her with a gun. Mitchell agreed to attend domestic violence counseling as part of the settlement.

Following his MVP season, Mitchell posted solid but lower numbers in 1990: .290, 35 homers and 93 RBIs. His performance dropped precipitously in 1991, as Mitchell batted .256 with 27 homers and 69 RBIs.

Mitchell aggravated Giants management by missing workouts, arriving late at Spring Training, and suffering frequent injuries.

Mitchell faced another legal struggle in 1991, when police arrested him for rape, though he said the woman who accused him was retaliating against him for dumping her. "They were trying to give me nine years, and a $750,000 fine, all because I was leaving her," Mitchell said. After the woman decided not to testify, prosecutors dropped the charges against him.

Giants general manager Al Rosen decided to deal Mitchell two days later. On December 11, 1991, the Giants sent Mitchell and pitcher Mike Remlinger to Seattle for pitchers Bill Swift, Mike Jackson and Dave Burba.

Mitchell was unhappy to leave the Giants, the team he still associates with more than any of his seven other big league clubs.

"The Giants have been such an awesome team for me," Mitchell said. "They've always been my team, and they're still my team. I've still got relationships with the players there."

Mitchell's following years with the Mariners, Reds, the Japanese Fukuoka Daiei Hawks, the Red Sox, Indians and Athletics featured spectacular highlights. He hit a grand slam in his first at-bat in Japan, batted .341 with the Reds in 1993 and hit 30 home runs for Cincinnati in the strike-shortened 1994 season.

He also suffered an absurd rash of injuries, and never played again in as many as 100 games in a season. He once burned his eyes with rubbing alcohol, strained rib muscles while vomiting and somehow hurt a tooth while eating a donut.

Then there were the scuffles and bouts with management. Mitchell had a shouting match with Reds manager Davey Johnson in 1994. He abandoned the Japanese Daiei Hawks midseason in 1995 because they disagreed about the severity of a knee injury. The Reds suspended Mitchell in 1996 after he failed to report for a series in Pittsburgh. A fight with Cleveland teammate Chad Curtis landed Curtis on the disabled list and preceded the Indians' cutting Mitchell in 1997.

The press reported every incident, sometimes in a mocking tone. "He is the Wile. E. Coyote of baseball," wrote *Sports Illustrated's* Tom Verducci. "He keeps falling off cliffs, getting conked on the head with anvils, opening packages that explode and, inevitably, coming back for more."

That kind of attention didn't bother him, Mitchell said.

"I grew up in the streets, where all they ever do is talk about people," Mitchell said. "I used to tell the press, 'You can talk about me all you want. All you're doing is making me famous.' Jim Rome would talk about me every day. Those people don't know me, so I don't worry about it. When I got to worry is when they stop talking."

Night-vision goggles and a seven-foot boa were a few of the things he used to liven up the clubhouse.

"Back in those days, I was wild," Mitchell admitted.

But his life was about to drastically change.

✸ ✸ ✸ ✸ ✸ ✸ ✸

Mitchell's jet ski accident occurred prior to his 1998 season with the Oakland Athletics. As he floated on an innertube near his home at Lake Havasu, a young jet skier, possibly intoxicated, smashed into his side.

"He came out of nowhere. I didn't even see him coming," Mitchell said. "It shoved my pancreas down, and messed up my kidneys. The innertube saved my head."

The young jet skier fled the scene, and Mitchell was flown by emergency helicopter to a Phoenix hospital. A doctor described his internal injuries, prompting Mitchell to ask, "Can I buy a new pancreas?" The doctor told him no.

The hospital released him, and Mitchell reported to Spring Training, but he didn't discover that his pancreas injury had caused him diabetes until much later.

"I knew something was wrong with me. I was always tired and thirsty, shooting a lot of [vitamin] B12," he said. "I thought I might have cancer."

Mitchell stuck with it past the All-Star break, batting .228 with two home runs in 51 games as Oakland's designated hitter. Fastballs flew past his head that he didn't even see. He was not playing the game like Kevin Mitchell, and nobody knew why, not even him.

"People thought he was out of shape, he put on too much weight, his bat speed was disappearing," said Steve Bitker, a KCBS radio sportscaster who also announced games for the Sonoma Crushers of the independent Western League. In that capacity, Bitker got to know Mitchell when the slugger joined the Crushers in 2000.

"They thought he was done, a former slugger who let his body dissipate, and he disappeared from the radar amid scorn and ridicule," Bitker said. "As it turns out, it was through no fault of his own."

Mitchell asked for his release. On August 7, 1998, the Athletics obliged him.

"My mind was telling me I could still play, but my body wasn't," Mitchell said. "I went from 263 [pounds] to 202 in three weeks. I had to find out what was wrong. I got home and went to the doctor. My sugar level was bad, my eyesight was bad. Thank God I wasn't still out there playing every day. I learned so much about diabetes, which I didn't know nothing about."

Over time, Mitchell learned to tame his diabetes with insulin shots four times per day. Later he learned to get by with insulin tablets and an altered diet: lots of vegetables, water, and nothing with much sugar. "Thank God I was able to get off the needles," he said. But though he would play again and later manage in the Western League, Mitchell's big league career ended at age 36.

"I still think about it sometimes and it pisses me off, because [the jet skier] hit me and kept going," Mitchell said. "It messed up my play. I regret that I left the game the way I did.

"But the doctor said if I wasn't as thick as I was, I'd probably be dead," he said. "I sat in the hospital and thought about a lot of things. It changed my life. I've been blessed. I think He did it for a reason, to slow me down."

✿ ✿ ✿ ✿ ✿ ✿

Mitchell joined the Sonoma Crushers in 2000, when his old Giants team-mate Jeffrey "Hac Man" Leonard managed the team. Mitchell played in 45 games for the Crushers in 2000, hitting .286 with seven home runs and 34 RBIs.

"Mitch was amazing," recalled Bitker. "A lot of times former major leaguers do not adapt well to playing in independent leagues like the Western League. The long bus rides, minimal pay, and conditions are so foreign to what they are accustomed to. Most don't last long, and some quit before the first game.

"There were some skeptics when he showed up, although in many respects he was a changed individual because of his life-threatening battle with diabetes," Bitker said. "He nearly died before he was diagnosed, which may have made him appreciate things he had taken for granted before."

Yet the physical effects of playing through his diabetes took their toll.

"He had a lot of difficulty getting his meds in tune with his blood sugar," said Crushers owner Bob Fletcher. "He was trying to do that and to make a come-back after not playing for a couple of years.

"When he hit them, they went like shots, no question, though he didn't real-ly tear up the league like we all hoped he would," Fletcher said. "He had to miss a lot of games, but he always had a great attitude and was good in the club-house."

After leading the Crushers to a 38-52 season, Leonard left the team and in 2003 became the head coach of Antelope Valley College's baseball team in Southern California.

Mitchell retired from playing but stayed with the Crushers as a coach in 2001 and became the team's skipper in 2002.

"He loved it, and we love Kevin to death. We still stay in touch with him," Fletcher said.

Mitchell called his year at the Crushers' helm "the most enjoyable time I had in my career." He led the Crushers to a 49-41 record in 2002, the last year the Western League existed.

As a manager, Mitchell drew favorable comparisons to longtime Giants skip-per Dusty Baker from Crushers broadcaster Steve Wendt.

"I thought he had a real good relationship with players. He was like Dusty Baker in that regard," Wendt said. "He'd buck the odds, go against the book and put his faith in his guys. Sometimes it worked out, and sometimes it didn't. The hitters liked it because he didn't take the bat out of their hands. He let his bop-pers bop, and didn't play a lot of small ball.

"He never put his guys in situations to fail," Wendt added. "He did a good job of knowing who he had and doing his best to minimize exposing the weak-nesses."

However, the league twice suspended Mitchell for brawling on the field.

"We had some challenging situations," Fletcher said. "Kevin had a difficult upbringing that sometimes colors his outlook and his response to adversity."

For instance, the league suspended Mitchell for eight games in 2000 following a fracas with Solano Steelheads owner Bruce Portner. In a tense game in which both sides accused the other of throwing at batters, former major leaguer Jim Converse threw behind the head of Mitchell, who charged the mound and landed a few blows.

"Kevin is very strong, and if he wanted to do real damage, he could," said Fletcher. "He got tossed. That's the way it goes. It happens. I don't think anybody in baseball is proud when it happens, in contrast to hockey.

"It should have ended there, but [Portner] went out to the field, wagging his finger at Kevin," Fletcher said. "[Portner] had no business being out there. Kevin didn't know him, and thought he was a fan. Kevin gave him a good slap and knocked him down."

Two years later as the team's manager, Mitchell was suspended for seven games for striking the Steelheads' third base coach, Larry Olenberger. Mitchell accused Olenberger of leaving the coach's box to steal signs from the Crushers' catcher and relaying them to the Steelheads' hitters.

Both events drew national media attention. Portner demanded that the league permanently expel Mitchell. Yet Mitchell was the league's biggest star who spent hours signing autographs for children.

"I have very rarely seen a bigger chasm between a guy's public persona and the way he actually is," said Wendt. "He was a real ambassador who did as much to keep the league alive as long as it was as anybody else, those ugly incidents aside."

The Western League's financial challenges became critical prior to the 2003 season. The league experienced 27 team and ownership changes in an eight-year span and never achieved financial stability. The remaining owners decided to shut it down.

"There was no way we could go forward," Fletcher said. "There were some efforts to sustain the league, but all efforts eventually failed. In some ways, it's remarkable that the league lasted 10 years."

Mitchell returned home to San Diego, where he quickly found new challenges.

* * * * * * *

Gang members today call him "O.G.," short for old gangster. Mitchell received three gunshot wounds while growing up on San Diego's tough streets and knows how dangerous the gang scene can be.

Now in the graffiti-covered neighborhood where he grew up, Mitchell tries to point gang members and wannabes in their bright white T-shirts and sagging pants in a better direction. He volunteers for Black Men United, a group created to "stop the violence and stop the killing," says Mitchell.

Black Men United formed in response to youth violence and other community problems in San Diego. Though its name describes its founding members, the coalition has grown to include men and women of many ethnicities drawn

*Mitchell overcame diabetes, managed a
minor league team and became a single father.*
Photo by Matt Johanson

from community groups, like the YMCA, NAACP, the Urban League, the Police
Department, and churches.

"We broke down the barriers," says the group's founder, Reverend Ricky Laster.
"We said, 'Let's leave religion and all that stuff at the door. We've got kids killing
kids; we've got to come together. Check the egos, let's go.' It was the first time we've
ever had this kind of diversity. There's some of everybody for one cause."

Black Men United has raised reward money to help the police solve murders,
and contributed money towards the burials of poor murder victims. The group
provides mentoring, counseling and job placement assistance to young people,

"from teenagers all the way up to guys who have done 10 to 15 years in prison and are trying to start over," Laster said.

Mitchell calls Laster his mentor and the Martin Luther King, Jr. of southeast San Diego. Laster credits Mitchell as an invaluable role model.

"When our kids see somebody like Kevin Mitchell, a Major League Baseball player and MVP from their neighborhood, he gives hope to them," says Laster. "They see that they too can be what God wants them to be. It's not like watching an MTV video of somebody that's not really real. Kevin's real life. They can talk to him when they have some questions. He's done an awesome job in the community."

Mitchell's other focus is his daughter and her half-sister. Their mother is addicted to crystal methamphetamine, Mitchell says, and despite the $6,000 monthly child support he gave her, she lived with the girls in a shelter. In 2003, Mitchell sought and received custody of both girls, so they wouldn't be separated.

"She's been a handful, because her mom just let her do whatever she wanted to do," Mitchell says of his daughter. "I'm trying to break all that."

Living off of his baseball money and the income from his Home Run Hair Design beauty parlors, Mitchell can spend much of his time with the girls. Part of that means keeping close tabs on his daughter's progress at school; his support is a teacher's dream.

"When her teacher calls me from school, I go up there banging," Mitchell says. "She knows I'm coming to get on her. I'll embarrass her in front of all her classmates. ... If you want anything in life, it's not going to come to you. You got to go get it.

"She understands what's going on now," Mitchell says. "She's going to miss her mom. I understand that. I tell her, 'When your mom gets right, I'll let you see your mom.' I pray to God that she does, because it ain't good, a girl without her mother."

While the girls' lives have changed, parenthood has changed Mitchell himself, "especially with women," he says. "I can't be bringing just any woman in my home around these girls." The former baseball playboy even talks of marriage, if he finds the right woman who will accept his girls.

"He takes care of everybody," says Baker. "He takes care of his family, his mom and dad, grandma, his daughters, half the neighborhood. Mitch is a giver. He's not a taker. He has the kindest heart. He's the biggest hearted guy I've met."

Can Kevin Mitchell the community volunteer and parent really replace Kevin Mitchell the wildly talented but wild slugger?

Mitchell says it was meant to happen. "The Lord had a plan for me to come out here and work with these kids," he said.

BOB LURIE

"It Was Time to Move On"

A t least Bob Lurie can laugh at himself. In his downtown San Francisco office, on a wall covered with Giants memorabilia, sits a framed cartoon of a Giants player. On his jersey are the names of several cities, one on top of another. San Francisco, Santa Clara, and San Jose are all crossed out. Beneath them all, San Francisco's unmarred name appears a second time.

More than a decade has passed since Lurie lost his fourth ballot measure to build a new ballpark, a loss so demoralizing that he nearly sold the team to Florida investors who planned to move the team to Tampa Bay.

When Lurie's flirtation with Florida became public, the local news media ridiculed and skewered him, forgetting that he had saved the Giants from moving to Toronto when he bought the team in 1976.

"Bob Lurie has kicked his hometown by the teeth," wrote Glenn Dickey of the *San Francisco Chronicle*. "Lurie is acting like a petulant child, trying to punish us because he didn't get what he wanted." Ray Ratto, then of the *San Francisco Examiner*, was more succinct, calling Lurie, "The new Public Enemy No. 1."

Since selling the team in 1993, Lurie has kept out of the spotlight, but is still active in the community as he quietly oversees his real estate empire and manages the foundation his father created, doling out an average of $2 million a year to Bay Area charities. Despite the rocky ending to his tenure as Giants owner, ask Lurie today about his 17 years of ownership and he will tell you, "It was a fabulous experience. No regrets."

Lurie remains a Giants fan. He just roots for them from afar. Even though he's a charter seat holder at AT&T Park with seats behind the dugout, he attends only a few games a year. The rest of his tickets he gives to employees and friends.

"I saw a lot of games the first year [after selling the team], but it's been less

Bob Lurie bought the Giants in 1976, preventing a move to Toronto.
© S.F. Giants

each year," said Lurie, from his 51st-floor office on California Street. "I still follow them. I listen to them. I read about them in the paper."

Selling the team was an easy decision after losing the final ballot measure in San Jose in 1992, said Lurie, who for years blamed the cold, windy conditions at Candlestick for the team's inability to attract fans.

"When we lost our last ballot, that's when I decided it was enough. I loved the game. I loved the experience. But I wanted to get out," Lurie said. "It got to the point that it wasn't that hard a decision. It was a relief. People, starting with my wife, going on down, were emotionally concerned because I was so involved. It was time to move on."

Lurie, a private man, doesn't like to talk about himself. After years in the public eye, Lurie now prefers anonymity. He's succeeded in that effort, except for an occasional mention of him and his wife Connie in the local society columns. Giants owner or not, he remains a mover-and-shaker in San Francisco.

In late 2003, he retired as president of The Lurie Co., handing over the reins of his private real estate company to his long-time business associate Gene Vallo. Lurie, who took over the helm in 1972 when his father died, remains as chairman. He still arrives at his office at the Bank of America building early in the morning, sometimes staying until 5 P.M. He'll cut out early several times a week to golf.

"I still get up early and get here at 7:30 or 8 in the morning. You get into bad habits. You like them and you keep them," said Lurie, dressed in a dapper suit on this cold, rainy winter afternoon. "I'm involved with operations. They're just not as complex as they were before. Gene is doing more day to day stuff. We talk every day about any projects, any problems. We own a lot of office buildings of varying sizes, but we're not as active as we used to be. We're kind of calming things down."

Lurie is busy with the Lurie Foundation, a charity that gives grants to mostly Bay Area and Chicago organizations that benefit youth. He and foundation board members visit every agency before making grants, which range from $2,500 to $30,000 a year. Recent beneficiaries include the San Francisco Symphony, which has a youth orchestra that performs in grammar schools, to Huckleberry House, which provides haven and services for at-risk, homeless, and runaway youth in San Francisco. The education center at the San Francisco Zoo even bears the name of Bob and Connie Lurie.

"We spend a lot of time screening each organization," Lurie said. "They're all good causes—educational, medical, and cultural. We've gotten involved with child abuse programs. If you visit some of those places, it's really dramatic."

As his wall of baseball mementos can attest, Lurie is fond of his time with the Giants. Near his office window, which features a picturesque view of San Francisco Bay and the Bay Bridge, is a wall of framed memorabilia that includes a baseball bat, team pins, and the lineup cards from Game 5 of the 1989

National League Championship game between the Giants and Cubs, the day the Giants won the pennant with Will Clark's late-inning heroics.

"The '78 team was excellent. We had some great talent and got really close, but '87 and '89 were better," Lurie said. "There's nothing like the excitement of winning and getting to the World Series. Those were exciting times. As Al Rosen used to say, 'Baseball in October is the best.'"

Lurie, a father of six children, grew up loving baseball, having played the outfield in grammar and high school in the San Francisco Peninsula, and rooting on the DiMaggio brothers and the rest of the Minor League's San Francisco Seals at Seals Stadium.

He bought the Giants in 1976 because he felt it was his civic duty to keep Major League Baseball in San Francisco. Then-owner Horace Stoneham, who had moved the Giants from New York to San Francisco in 1958, was cash-strapped after two straight seasons of drawing only about 500,000 fans to Candlestick. So he sold the team to Labatt's Breweries of Toronto, which planned to move the team to Canada. Then-Mayor George Moscone got a temporary injunction that prevented the sale, which bought him some time to find local investors.

Lurie stepped up to the plate.

He recalls getting on a conference call with Major League Baseball team owners, telling them he was interested in buying the Giants, but that he needed 48 hours to find a business partner to share the cost. The team owners responded by giving him five hours, or else the team would move to Toronto.

"A lot of owners wanted to see the Giants leave Candlestick. They didn't like the park, so they were happy with the prospect with the Giants moving to Toronto," recalled Lurie. "So in their great wisdom, they gave me five hours."

With a 5 P.M. deadline looming, Lurie quickly called up other affluent San Franciscans. "There were a lot of people in town who said, 'If you ever want to be involved with the Giants, we'd love to be a part of it, and call me,'" Lurie said. "My bottom line: when I called them, they were all out to lunch."

An Arizona cattleman named Bob Herseth called Mayor Moscone's office, which quickly put him in touch with Lurie. At 5 P.M., Lurie told the Major League team owners that he had a partner and was ready to offer $8 million for the Giants.

"[Dodgers owner] Walter O'Malley was the biggest help," Lurie recalled. "He didn't want to see the rivalry disappear, so at that conference call, he did a nice sales pitch and said, 'Let's keep the Giants where they are.'"

The Giants were saved, and Lurie was the savior. "I was a hero until we lost our first few games," he joked.

As team owner, Lurie watched more than 110 games a year at Spring Training, at Candlestick, and even on the road. He'd take care of his real estate business in the morning, then drive to Candlestick to oversee the Giants.

Lurie was a hands-off owner, letting the general manager, scouting staff, manager, and coaches run the show. He would, on occasion, sit in on contract negotiations, if he felt his presence would help. When he hired Rosen as president and general manager late in the 1985 season, he told Rosen: "I want to know what you're thinking before I read about it in the paper."

Lurie, who in 1977 bought out Herseth's share of the Giants, spent considerable time and money trying to convince the public to give him public money to build a new Giants ballpark. Like Stoneham before him, Lurie was tired of losing money. With the average player salary growing from $58,000 when he bought the team to $1.1 million by the early 1990s, he knew the Giants would lose money as long as they stayed at Candlestick.

"Normally, when you take a survey, asking, 'Why didn't you go to the ballgame?' it's because the team isn't winning," said Lurie, who lost money from yearly operations during his 17 years as owner. "At Candlestick, it was because 'We don't like the ballpark.' That was more important than winning and losing."

Throughout the 1980s, he threatened to move or sell the team if San Francisco didn't build him a new ballpark. There was talk of building a dome over Candlestick, or constructing a new domed stadium in downtown San Francisco.

In one of the more embarrassing moments of Lurie's ownership, he and then-San Francisco Mayor Dianne Feinstein announced in a press conference in 1985 a plan for the Giants to temporarily share the Oakland Coliseum with the Oakland A's, a plan that Oakland Mayor Lionel Wilson criticized, and the Coliseum's Board of Directors rejected.

"The San Francisco Giants will not, under my ownership, play at Candlestick beyond this season," Lurie said in an October 1985 press conference. A few months later, Lurie announced the team would remain at Candlestick as part of a new effort to build a ballpark in downtown San Francisco.

From 1987 to 1992, he made four attempts to secure public money to build a new stadium—twice in San Francisco and once each in Santa Clara and San Jose. Voters turned him down each time. He had a near-miss in '89 when San Francisco voters rejected a new stadium by 1,800 votes.

Given the go-ahead by baseball's commissioner to explore the sale of the team, Lurie in August 1992 announced an agreement to sell the team for $115 million to a Florida group that would move the team to the St. Petersburg-Tampa Bay area.

"The group came in from Florida with an offer that you can't refuse. It was unbelievable," he recalled. "I talked to the league president, the commissioner, every owner in the National League at least twice and every owner in the American League at least once, as to what the situation was and what was happening. If anybody comes along and wants to keep the club in San Francisco that's fine. I told [the Florida group], 'If we can come to an understanding, and make an agreement, if someone locally comes, you're out.'"

The sale and move to Florida looked like a done deal, but team owners held off voting on the deal for months, until San Francisco investors, led by Peter Magowan, came up with a $95 million to $100 million offer.

Lurie is vague on details, but said the backroom politics that ensued after the Florida deal was struck disturbed him.

"It ended up with some of the owners saying one thing to me, and then doing other things," he said. "All I wanted was an honest answer. There are some people who go through life who will tell you one thing, and walk out the door and tell someone else something different. We ran into some of that, which is a major disappointment, considering who some of these people are."

Nevertheless, Lurie said he was happy the team stayed in San Francisco, even though he could have made more money on the Florida deal.

"They stayed here, so that was more important," he said.

He credits Magowan and the rest of the current Giants management for building AT&T Park. In the team's fifth attempt at a ballpark ballot measure, San Francisco voters approved the deal, in large part because it was privately financed.

"I think the park is outstanding and they did a terrific job," he said.

Lurie feels the media unfairly vilified him for nearly moving the team to Florida.

"Most of the writers have maintained their professional distance... Not me. I wanted to kill somebody on August 7, the day Lurie sold us down the river," wrote *San Francisco Chronicle* columnist Bruce Jenkins. "I'm right there with the common folk in taverns from Novato to Los Gatos, screaming into their shot glasses. They don't want to hear the rationale behind this move, because there isn't any. If Lurie gets his way, the Bay Area loses the Giants. We're supposed to feel sympathy for this man? A guy who didn't get the palace, so he just turned and ran? Take your idiot rationalizations somewhere else."

"It hasn't helped... that Lurie has been saying for years that Candlestick is not fit for baseball," added Dickey in the *Chronicle*. "Neiman-Marcus probably wouldn't prosper if it ran ads telling potential customers how awful it was inside their store."

The press called Lurie a traitor, but could their personal stake have colored their reporting? "If the Giants went to Florida, they might lose their jobs, so there was some of that," Lurie said.

Months after the sale, Lurie felt deep regret for selling the team, recalls Vallo, his business partner. In early 1993, the Lurie Co. purchased a table for an annual Giants fund-raising luncheon like it did every year. But this time, Lurie didn't want to go. "He had seller's remorse," Vallo said. "He was emotionally bothered by the fact that he was no longer connected to the team."

Through Vallo's urging, however, Lurie attended the event and was overwhelmed by compliments from fans, players, coaches, and ballpark employees.

"He couldn't get through the door without people saying thanks," Vallo said. "The fans, the players, and coaches all knew the rollercoaster ride. They threw

Lurie still enjoys the baseball glove chair in his downtown San Francisco office.
Photo by Matt Johanson

nothing but accolades and positive comments. And it came from the people who counted, not some bloody guy in Major League Baseball who twisted the truth or sportswriters writing whatever they wanted to sell papers."

After the luncheon, Lurie felt closure and was able to move on with his life, Vallo added. "The remorse was lifted. He was free. It was like the gates of freedom were open at last."

Since retiring, when he's not doing his philanthropic work, Lurie and his wife enjoy traveling. Recent destinations include Europe, Hawaii and Charleston, South Carolina.

He's also a 49ers fan, with season tickets since the team played in Kezar Stadium, though he doesn't make it out to games much anymore. "I've spent enough time at Candlestick," he joked.

Some people may have forgotten that he once saved the Giants, but not everybody. How will Giants fans remember him? Lurie chuckled as he pondered the answer.

"Hopefully in a positive light," he said. "Things have calmed down. I still hear it, not on a daily basis or regularly, but people say, 'Thanks for saving the team.' I appreciate that. People do remember."

ROGER CRAIG

TIGER TRAINER

Roger Craig was back in baseball, doing the one thing he loved: tutoring pitchers and teaching them the split-finger fastball.

In 2003 and 2004, the San Francisco Giants manager coached the Detroit Tigers during Spring Training and consulted for the team during the season. He worked with pitchers and provided advice on baseball strategy to then-Tigers manager Alan Trammell and the coaching staff for about two weeks in the preseason. When the season started, he analyzed the Tigers pitchers on TV, and sometimes behind home plate at Comerica Park, gave pitching tips and feedback to the coaches.

Craig began working for the Tigers at Trammell's request. Trammell was a new manager at the time and wanted his former coach on hand to give feedback during his first Spring Training. Craig served a similar role for his protégé Bob Brenly during the former Giants catcher's first three seasons as the Arizona Diamondbacks' manager, from 2001 to 2003.

Craig, who began his playing career with the Brooklyn Dodgers in 1955, relishes his role as mentor to a new generation of pitchers, managers and coaches.

"I've been in baseball—teaching—all my life. When you get to my age, it's nice to be invited back in the major leagues to work with teams. I feel complimented," Craig said.

During Spring Training in 2003, Craig split time between the Diamondbacks and Tigers, and very nearly coached a third team, the Seattle Mariners. It was former Giants catcher Bob Melvin's first year as the Mariners' manager and he wanted to tap into Craig's expertise, but then-general manager Pat Gillick squelched the idea because Craig was already working for the competition.

But the fact that his former players who have become big league managers are seeking his advice and support says a lot about Craig and his impact when he was

Roger Craig led the Giants to the World Series in 1989.
Brace Photo

pitching coach for the Tigers from 1980 to 1984, and when he was the Giants manager from the end of the 1985 season through 1992.

Current and former players alike say Craig's vast knowledge of the game makes him a great mentor. But what sets him apart from other coaches and managers is his positive thinking and his unwavering belief in his players that helps them build their own self confidence.

Kirk Gibson credits Craig for his major turnaround after having a dismal 1983 season, when he hit .227. Manager Sparky Anderson considered using Gibson as a part-time outfielder. Craig, then the pitching coach, lobbied Anderson to play him every day. With Craig's support, Gibson rebounded in 1984 with a .282 average with 27 homers and 91 RBIs, leading the Tigers to the World Series title.

"In 1983, I had a really bad year. When I came back in 1984, he would hit me fungoes every day in right field. He used to always go fight for me to Sparky to play every day. He used to say, 'If you don't play this kid every day, I'm quitting,'" Gibson said. "He knew I had a lot of ability and saw that I was struggling. Every day, he talked about 'I can do it. I can do it.' And it came true."

Former Giants owner Bob Lurie recalls Craig's first speech to the Giants players when he became San Francisco's manager near the end of the 1985 season. He made an immediate impact in the clubhouse, turning around a lifeless franchise that lost 100 games in 1985 and made it proud once again, capturing the National League West tile in 1987 and the pennant in 1989.

"When Al introduced Roger, you could see all the players sitting back. They've heard all the baloney from a new manager before. And Roger kept talking, and by the end, they were all sitting up and paying attention," Lurie said. "Every manager knows the game of baseball. They might approach it different a little bit as far as strategy, but to motivate players over a long period of time takes personality. He had that motivational ability."

Craig regularly told Giants players to stop complaining about the weather at Candlestick Park. Every visiting team hates the ballpark and just wants to play its three games and move on, he told the players. "We know the park, the wind, so let's take advantage of that and win. It was one of those motivational things, and we played well for a lot of years."

Craig, who had an up-and-down pitching career, wanted to stay in baseball and become a pitching coach when his playing days were over. His best season was in 1959, going 11-5 with a 2.06 ERA as Los Angeles captured the World Series crown. In his 12-year career, he played for five teams and got three World Series rings. He won two World Series games, once for Brooklyn in 1955 and once for the Cardinals in 1964.

After spending his first seven seasons as a Dodger, Craig was drafted by the expansion New York Mets in 1962, where he was the franchise's first Opening Day starter. He was 10-22 for a team that went a dismal 40-120 in its inaugural year. He lost 24 more games the next year despite a respectable 3.78 ERA, as he became the first National Leaguer ever to lead the league in losses for two straight years. Then he bounced from St. Louis and Cincinnati to Philadelphia in his last three seasons, retiring at age 36.

"As my career was winding down, I went to all the great pitchers and managers and asked questions and prepared myself to be a pitching coach," he said.

Craig said he loved coaching pitchers so much, he never considered managing. But when presented with the opportunity, he took it, first with the San Diego Padres in 1978 and 1979, then with San Francisco when Lurie and Rosen approached him.

The Giants players, the fans and even the media embraced Craig, who turned the team into a winner. He taught the entire pitching staff—from Scott Garrelts to Kelly Downs—his famous split-finger fastball, which earlier turned Houston's Mike Scott and Detroit's Jack Morris into dominating 20-game winners. Soon after, Craig single-handedly made the split-finger the in-vogue pitch of the '80s and his slogan, "Humm Baby," a rallying cry for the up-and-coming young team that quickly became one of the National League's best.

"Roger Craig came in and changed the personnel, and more than anything else, changed the attitude of the ballclub," Brenly said. "I bought into the whole schtick—Humm Baby and his positive attitude every day. And I know a lot of other players bought into it, too."

Turning San Francisco into a winner was the highlight of his baseball career, Craig said.

"We didn't have a lot of big-name players," Craig said. "But we had youngsters like Will Clark, Matt Williams, and Robby Thompson, and the next year, we were in the playoffs."

Craig loved to play hunches while managing the Giants, and more often than not, those hunches worked, Williams said.

"It was uncanny. He would put a hit-and-run on, with guys on first and second and nobody out, and it would work. He knew it would work. It was an educated hunch," Williams said.

Craig's hunches worked because he knew the Giants hitters, but he also knew the opposition's pitchers and their defense, Williams said. "You would sit on the bench and go, 'How do you know that?' It was from being around the game for so long. He liked his matchups, and knew his matchups, but also liked to play hunches, too. It was very successful for him."

Craig, who had a penchant for the suicide squeeze, said he's still surprised that his "Humm Baby" slogan took off the way it did. To this day, when he runs into former players like Brenly, their first words to Craig are, "Humm Baby." Dave Dravecky simply calls him, "Humm."

The slogan has many different meanings. He first began using the slogan while growing up and playing baseball with other kids. At that time, Craig was a shortstop. "When we played behind the pitcher, we said, 'C'mon, baby! Let's go! C'mon baby!,'" Craig said. "And when the pitcher went into the windup and was about to throw, you say it fast, 'Humm Baby!'"

By the time he became manager of the Giants, he used the slogan as a positive term for everything. "I would say, 'That's a Humm Baby play,' or 'That's a Humm Baby pitch,' or 'That good-looking girl? Now, that's a real Humm Baby,'" he said. "I don't know how it took off in San Francisco, but you heard it on the radio, and on TV, and on the scoreboard. It was a positive thing."

Despite knee replacement surgery in recent years, Craig can still get around. During the summer of 2004, Craig had a busy travel schedule. In June, he flew to Detroit for a 20th anniversary celebration of the Tigers' 1984 World Series win. Then in July, he flew to California for his granddaughter's wedding.

Earlier in the year, Craig had a bout of pneumonia that sent him to a hospital emergency room, but he fully recovered, feeling good and playing golf almost every day.

He and his wife Carolyn live in a home that's right on a golf course in Borrego Springs, California, the San Diego area.

Tigers players and coaches say Craig's insight and keen eye helped the team tremendously. During the 2004 season, Craig watched the Tigers' pitchers from behind home plate for about 10 games at Comerica Park, then he gave Tigers pitching coach Bob Cluck a full scouting report. The two are old friends and co-owned a youth baseball academy in San Diego.

"I work with the pitchers before the game, and go and sit behind home plate and observe what they're doing and what they're not doing, then I relay that stuff to the pitching coach," Craig said.

When he can't make it to the Detroit, he watches games on TV. One time, Craig watched young starter Jeremy Bonderman on TV and was troubled by his pitching tendencies. He noticed that Bonderman had a penchant for throwing fastballs on certain counts and curveballs on certain counts.

"Roger picked that up on the TV, watching a game and said, 'Hey, do you realize he's becoming predictable?'" Cluck recalled. "And hey, things slip by you when you're watching a game. You don't see everything. You're watching mechanics... To be honest, you have a lousy view from the dugout. So he'll see things at home and call me and put me onto something, and I'll go check it out."

Craig has helped the Tigers young pitching staff mature, particularly Bonderman, who was a 20-year-old rookie in 2003. That spring, Craig helped improve Bonderman's curveball, changeup, and fastball—and even taught him the split-finger, which Bonderman had used on occasion. After making the team that spring, Bonderman honored Craig by choosing Craig's old number 38 for his jersey.

"Roger's contribution is being positive and showing guys how to compete," Cluck said. "He has sayings like, 'You start every game like you're going to throw a no-hitter. And if you give up one hit, then you're going to throw a one-hit shutout,' and so you keep motivating yourself. And if you give up three runs in the first inning, you come into the dugout and say, 'I'm going to win this game 4-3.' So that's his philosophy: That every game is going to be a perfect game until something happens, and then you keep re-establishing your goals throughout the game and beat them."

When Trammell was a rookie manager in 2003, Craig took him and the other coaches aside and gave them lessons on baseball strategy, and also the roles of each of the coaches.

"I first talked about what the manager expected from them individually. They all had a job to do and not to interfere with other people's jobs," Craig said.

He also told the coaches to say what's on their mind before the game or during the game, and not second guess the manager after the fact. "The manager wants to know before it happens. If you have something to say before the game or during the game, say it," Craig added. "Don't say, 'We should have done this or that' after the game."

When Brenly won the World Series after his first season with the Diamondbacks, he gave Craig a World Series ring not only for his contributions to the team, but as a thank you for mentoring him. Craig, he said, was a terrific presence for players and coaches during Spring Training.

"We brought him down to Tucson and had him work with some of our young pitchers, and more than anything else, just to be around that positive attitude. It's infectious and rubs off on guys," Brenly said. "He's so happy to be in the ballpark, and even the most innocuous infield drill that every team does in spring training, he'd find a way to make it fun, and make you realize how important this really is. That this will help you win a game during the season."

Despite his age, Craig always had a knack for bonding with younger players, who are young enough to be his grandchildren.

"He understands people like no one I've ever known. He's very insightful and honest, so it doesn't take very long for people to warm up to Roger," Cluck said "To these guys, he's like grandpa. They love him for the stories about the Brooklyn Dodgers and all that."

Tiger reliever Jamie Walker said he enjoys hearing the old war stories from Craig, from stealing other team's signs, to the time Craig went to Spring Training with a broken left arm but played through it without telling anybody. "He's a throwback, a gamer. You don't see that attitude nowadays, and that's why I really like him," he said.

Craig has always been positive, but he was not afraid to yell at players when needed. He once scolded the Tigers' Walker during Spring Training when Walker tried to throw a ball as high as he could straight up in the air. "He isn't afraid to call you out and tell you the truth," Walker said. "I didn't even know he was watching me. He pulled me over and said, 'Boy, that's a good way to hurt your arm,' and cussed me out. I can respect that."

*Roger Craig comes out of retirement for several
weeks each spring to coach teams like the Detroit Tigers.*
Roger Craig family photo

After a brutal 43-119 season in 2003, the Tigers bounced back to respectabil-
ity in 2004, with the help of free agent pickups, such as catcher Ivan Rodriguez
and outfielder Rondell White, as well as via trades, such as shortstop Carlos
Guillen. The Tigers' young pitching staff also deserves some credit as its ERA
dropped from 5.30 in 2003 to just under 5.00 for most of the 2004 season.
"Because of the experience the young pitching had in 2003, they are a lot better," Craig said.

Craig, now in his early 80s, still roots for San Francisco. He has fond memories of throwing out the first pitch at AT&T Park during the World Series in

2002. Giants fans gave him a standing ovation, which made it a special, touching moment, Craig said.

"I went out to the mound, and I looked up and saw 40 to 50 signs with 'Humm Baby' on them," Craig recalled. "My son was with me in the dugout and he later said, 'His hair stood up with the fans cheering for me.'"

Craig's legacy in San Francisco is the fact that he restored pride in the Giants organization and got fans to come out to the ballpark in record numbers. After a 15-year drought, he took the team to the playoffs, and later to the World Series. Yet Craig deflects any praise, saying many people deserve the credit.

"I don't want to take credit for anything. I had a good relationship with the owner, the general manager and the players who played hard for me," he said. "And if I brought baseball back to San Francisco, that's good, but a lot of other people deserve that credit also. All I know is, when I go back there, it's almost like I never left. I love the city and the fans."

Craig is enjoying retired life and continues to be an avid golfer.

WILL
CLARK

"DADDY OF THE YEAR"

The announcement surprised many. When Will Clark retired from baseball at age 36, fresh off a .318 season and a deep playoff run, teammates and opponents alike knew "the Thrill" still had game. The St. Louis Cardinals, Clark's last team, wanted him back, and other clubs called his agent to express interest in the first baseman.

Clark had better things to do.

"The first part of my life was based on being a baseball player," explained Clark, a New Orleans native and wildly popular Giant for eight years. "The second part of my life is going to be based on being a daddy and a husband."

Clark and his wife Lisa had a baby boy, Trey, in the final years of his baseball career. Before long, they realized they faced an even greater challenge than most new parents.

"When Trey was two, he was starting to talk. Then he reverted and went the other way, to not talking at all," said Clark. "We knew there was something wrong."

The couple discovered that Trey suffers from autism, the brain disorder that inhibits one's ability to communicate or form relationships. They scrambled to get him as much help as possible while Clark maintained the punishing schedule of a Major League ballplayer.

"It wasn't easy, I can tell you that," Clark said. "I'd have to leave home and be away from him. My wife was in charge of taking care of him while I was gone. Now that I'm retired and home more, we see vast improvement in him."

When Clark arrived in San Francisco in 1986, the Giants had just suffered a last-place, 100-loss season, the worst in the franchise's 103 years. The team looked for a big contribution from Clark, winner of the Golden Spikes Award as the nation's best collegiate player and the Giants' top draft pick in 1985.

Will Clark's arrival in 1986 marked a
change of fortune for the struggling Giants.
© S.F. Giants

"He became the story of spring. It took a lot of pressure off of us," said teammate Mike Krukow. "We didn't have to have interviews talking about having lost 100 games. Because of that, there was no negativism in our camp that year. We got off to a great start and wound up turning our whole scenario around."

Clark didn't disappoint in his debut, smashing a home run in his first Major League at-bat off strikeout king Nolan Ryan.

"I thought I hit it pretty good," Clark said, "but when I came around first and looked up and saw it was gone, I said, 'Oh my goodness, no way.' I just floated around the rest of the base paths."

A veteran lineup in the Giants dugout tried not to look impressed, but Clark became an instant star, opening the season on a hot streak and hitting another home run in his first game at Candlestick Park. Catcher Bob Brenly gave him a catchy nickname: "Will the Thrill."

"His firsts were amazing," said Giants broadcaster Lon Simmons. "Every time he was going to have a first, he hit a home run. He was as good a pure hitter as there was around."

Clark hit .287 in his rookie season as the Giants rebounded, holding first place at the All-Star break. The fans loved his glare and his swagger. After Clark won a game at Candlestick with a walk-off homer, a fan held up a banner claiming "Will is God." Then a teammate placed a sign over his locker that said, "Once you realize I'm God, we'll get along fine." Clark just laughed.

"In those first couple of years, he was the heart and soul of the Giants," said former Giants broadcaster Ted Robinson. "In my nine years covering the Giants, Will was the Giants fans' greatest attraction."

When Clark improved to .308 and a career-best 35 home runs in 1987, he led the Giants to their first National League West title since 1971. As the Giants sprayed champagne in the clubhouse after clinching the championship, Clark showed his attitude that both thrilled and worried team officials. A television station broadcast the celebration live, and a reporter asked Clark how the victory felt. Clark shouted an expletive over the airwaves, loud and clear.

High-strung and competitive, Clark played with confidence, raw enthusiasm, and a game face set in stone. Sometimes he found it hard to set aside the intensity. Clark was known to shout profanities on the field after making outs at the plate. He also feuded with teammate Jeffrey Leonard, who angered Clark with his hazing. When Clark went on the disabled list as a rookie, Leonard dumped his bats in the garbage can. Teammates had to pull them apart after an explosive argument on another occasion.

The Giants traded Leonard to Milwaukee in 1988 and asked Clark to let off his steam out of earshot of the stands. Whatever problems arose around him were minor compared to his value to the club. In fact, Clark provided the inspiration for a team slogan: "I've got a Giant attitude." The Giants sold T-shirts sporting the motto and a picture of Clark's burning eyes.

"He had a high-squeaky voice, always making noise in the clubhouse," said former owner Bob Lurie. "Some players were bugged by it, but they always respected him because he played every inning like the World Series. He just didn't stop giving a 100 percent effort."

Clark gained a reputation as a tough-as-nails clutch hitter, especially in 1989. Clark hit .333 overall that season, but against the ten National League pitchers with the lowest ERAs, he hit .431. Against left-handers with runners in scoring position, the left-handed Clark hit an astonishing .450.

Clark dominated the 1989 National League Championship Series against the Chicago Cubs, setting five records for a five-game series with 13 hits, eight runs, 24 total bases, a .650 batting average, and a 1.200 slugging percentage. His grand slam off Greg Maddux propelled the Giants to a win in Game 1. But his at-bat in Game 5 against Mitch "Wild Thing" Williams was the one that cemented his place in Giants history. Clark came up in the bottom of the eighth in a tied game, with the bases loaded and two outs.

"His first pitch is a fastball, right on the outside corner," Clark recalled. "I said, 'Oh geez, of all the pitcher's pitches to make, the one I wanted to go get.' So I was in a hole, 0-1. Fastball up and I fouled it back, 0-2. He missed with a slider. Then he threw three straight fastballs up, and I fouled all of them off. The last one was damn near about head high, way up there, and I was fighting for my life. I wasn't going to give an inch, I was going to hang in here.

"Then the next pitch, still 1-2, was a fastball up, the same pitch I had just fouled off the pitch before. For some reason, I don't know how I did it, I got on top of it and hit a line drive back up the middle. Candy Maldonado scored, he was jumping on home plate, and Brett Butler came around and scored. I'm pointing in the dugout, I'm going crazy, [first base coach] Wendell Kim is giving me a hug."

San Francisco recorded the final out in the ninth inning on a ground ball to second baseman Robby Thompson, who fired to Clark at first. The Giants won their first pennant since 1962, although the Loma Prieta earthquake derailed the World Series.

The Giants rewarded Clark with a four-year, $15 million contract that made him the highest-paid player in baseball, even though he was two years away from free-agent eligibility. Clark was voted onto five consecutive All-Star teams from 1988 to 1992, although he declined offensively after the 1991 season.

Peter Magowan's ownership group took control of the team in 1993, hired Dusty Baker as manager, and signed then two-time MVP Barry Bonds. A furious pennant race broke out that year between the Giants and the Atlanta Braves.

"The sad part was in 1993 when Will wasn't the same player," Robinson said. "He didn't have long-term injuries. He just wasn't the same hitter. He hit for average. But he didn't hit for as much power as he did [in the past]."

Clark had a poor year at the plate by his standards, but caught fire during the last frantic days down the stretch. He hit a home run to beat San Diego in extra innings in a must-win September game. Calling the game on the radio, Robinson cried, "After 150 games, the Thrill is back in Candlestick." The ballpark erupted.

"You felt this incredible electricity," Robinson said. "The fans had been waiting all year for that dramatic moment. Barry had delivered most of them that year. Matt Williams delivered some, and Robby delivered some. But that was really the first time Will delivered that kind of moment that year where he won the game for the team."

In a dead heat, the Giants rode a winning streak into the season's last game in Los Angeles. Clark slapped eight hits in nine at-bats in the series, though the Dodgers roughed up rookie starter Salomon Torres en route to a blowout victory in the finale. San Francisco won 103 games, but fell one victory short of tying Atlanta and forcing a tiebreaker game. Clark ended the season with a .283 batting average and 14 home runs.

Clark's contract expired with the season's heartbreaking end. The Giants' contract with Bonds, six years for $43.7 million, made him the game's highest-paid player a year earlier. Clark expressed his desire to stay in San Francisco, but the team would not compete with the Texas Rangers' offer of five years for $30 million.

Asked in a radio interview why he didn't take the Giants' smaller offer, Clark replied, "I'm not stupid, okay?" He also told the audience, "In my heart, I will always be a Giant." With that, the Thrill was gone.

✿ ✿ ✿ ✿ ✿ ✿ ✿

Twenty-five feet up in a tree with a bow in one hand and a cell phone in the other, Clark announced his retirement from baseball in November 2000.

He had played seven more seasons with the Rangers, Orioles, and briefly the Cardinals, reaching the playoffs three times. But Clark had also suffered a long series of injuries, and had 36 bone chips removed from his left elbow from 1996 to 1999. Though he batted .345 in his final postseason with St. Louis just a month before, the Thrill decided 15 big league seasons were enough. He finished his career with a .303 batting average and 284 home runs.

"I was never of the opinion that I would play until every part of my body fell off," Clark told reporters from the treetop near his deer camp. "I can still hit, I can still play, I can still field my position. But also at the same time, this is the right time for me to exit."

The Thrill's early retirement enabled him to enjoy his outdoor interests. Clark grew up hunting and fishing with his father, and avidly continued both pursuits during his off-seasons and even on the occasional midseason holiday. Clark and Giants pitcher Mike LaCoss bagged three wild pigs in the middle of

Clark rejoined the Giants for a 2003 clinic at Pacific Bell Park.
Photo by Matt Johanson

the pennant race in 1989. An accomplished marksman with a bow or a firearm, Clark hunts "ducks, deer, turkeys, a bit of everything," he said, often near his home in the New Orleans area.

Clark kept his hand in baseball, assisting the Cubs and Cardinals in Spring Training, and appearing in 2004 at the Pro Series Baseball Camps in Marin, directed by his old teammate LaCoss.

Mainly, he tried to be "daddy of the year" to Trey and his younger sister, Ella, he said.

"Because of Trey's deficit in speech, we did a lot of speech pathology and other things related to try to get him talking. We tried going into a group setting, and getting him talking to other kids," Clark said.

"Autism comes in several different forms," he said. "There's the more severe 'Rain Man' type thing. Our son has gotten better to the point that he's having spontaneous conversations, so that's good."

Trey used to attend an autistic school, but improved enough to enter a mainstream Catholic school in New Orleans.

Unlike her older brother, Ella is prone to "non-stop talking," her father said. "She runs the show," said Clark. "Having a sister who talks so much now helps quite a bit."

After they discovered Trey's condition, the Clarks became active in supporting autism research, treatment and prevention through the National Alliance for Autism Research (NAAR). They helped promote an annual fundraiser dinner in New Orleans called "An Evening with Saints and Angels," along with such celebrities as author Anne Rice and television star John Goodman.

"We were new to the New Orleans area and people there didn't have a strong understanding of who we were," said NAAR's Joe Guzzardo. "Local folks like Will and Lisa were a great help in introducing the organization to community."

"The Thrill" also participated in a campaign to "strike out autism" in Minor League ballparks. Thirty teams agreed to donate some proceeds from their speed pitch booths to NAAR. Clark recorded a public service announcement and modeled for the promotional materials. The campaign raised $60,000 for the cause.

NAAR made the Clarks honorary board members, but Will went a step further in 2004. He created his own Will Clark Foundation to provide support not only for research but also to help autistic schools like the one Trey attended.

And finally Clark rejoined the Giants as a community ambassador and part-time coach in 2009, just in time to enjoy and contribute to the team's World Series championships in 2010 and 2012.

MATT WILLIAMS

WALK ON THE "POSITIVE" SIDE

Matt Williams was deep in thought as he leaned into the microphone. It's 5 P.M. on ESPN Radio 860 in Phoenix, and the topic of the day was the 2004 Summer Olympics in Greece: Are U.S. women athletes finally getting the media exposure they deserve?

"How about what they're wearing for volleyball?" asked host Roy Garibaldi, as he introduced the segment. "I've never enjoyed volleyball like I enjoyed it last night, I got news for you!"

"Fundamentally, that's wrong, Roy," scolded Williams, his co-host. "You are supposed to enjoy the sport, not what they wear."

Garibaldi was unapologetic. "I enjoyed both, thank you very much. I am human."

"I'm a true sports fan," Williams shot back.

"You're so full of crap," Garibaldi responded.

Welcome to "The Positive Side of Sports," a two-hour weekday talk show on ESPN affiliate KMVP in Phoenix. Williams, who majored in broadcasting in college, is the co-host two days a week. As the show's title suggests, it takes a different spin on sports, focusing on the good and not the negativity that permeates sports talk radio throughout the country.

"I love sports. What intrigues me is we show the other side. We give the insights of the athletes more than we do anything else, which is generally never talked about," said the former Giants and Diamondbacks player. "We talk about the good things athletes are doing in the community."

For example, the show recently announced that the Phoenix International Raceway was holding a fundraiser for two youngsters—a 13-year-old girl with leukemia and an 11-year-old boy with diabetes—to send them and their families to a summer camp. Garibaldi and Williams interviewed the two children as

Matt Williams hit 247 home runs in 10 seasons as a Giant.
Brace Photo

they called on listeners to donate money.

Williams, one of Arizona's most recognizable sports stars and starting third baseman for the 2001 World Series Champion Diamondbacks, feels comfortable in front of the microphone. "I've had a lot of experience, being asked the questions. I don't get nervous on air," he said. "I've embarrassed myself on the field enough to know that it's not that big a deal."

Williams, a five-time All Star who played third in ten years with the Giants, was a frequent guest on Garibaldi's show as a player, so when Williams retired midway through the 2003 season, Garibaldi asked him to join his show as a co-host.

The two are long-time friends, having met in the late 1980s when Garibaldi was the Giants' team photographer. Garibaldi, who also shot photos for the Oakland Athletics and other teams, got his radio show idea when he overheard players talk about how tough it was to deal with the media. He wanted to create a show to give athletes a chance to tell their side of the story. Now his creation is the top-rated show in Phoenix in its time slot.

Williams' public persona was that of a quiet, hard-nosed, competitive athlete. Now the public sees Williams in a different light—that he's got a sense of humor and has strong opinions on all sports, not just baseball.

"Like any other athlete, he's experienced it. There's nothing worse than to turn on the radio and listen to a bunch of wannabe jocks who pretend to know everything about sports. They've never taken the hit or made the free throws, and somehow they know everything," Garibaldi said. "Matt creates a different dimension. He's a Gold Glover, an All-Star and World Series champion. He's been on losing teams and winning teams."

Most of the time, Williams and Garibaldi have differing opinions, giving audiences a more sweeping view of the issues they discuss, Garibaldi said. That makes for entertaining and informative radio. After their sparring match over the wardrobe for women's volleyball, guest Amy Van Dyken, a five-time Olympic gold medalist swimmer, said anything that gets people watching or talking about women's sports is a good thing.

When Garibaldi asked about the female athletes who model for racy men's magazines, she said as long as photos are tastefully done, she approves.

"You work hard on your body. You look good and you want to show it off," she said, as the show was broadcast live on location from a Scottsdale restaurant. "A lot of times, as a female athlete, you struggle with that all your life. I'm in a boys' club, yet I'm very feminine. It's kind of a tug of war, and this is one way to show their femininity."

On another show, Williams debated Phoenix Suns broadcaster Eddie Johnson on whether team broadcasters should be critical. Williams said broadcasters should not criticize. His reasoning? If the team wins a World Series, the broadcasters get a ring, too.

Johnson said he has to criticize players for taking bad shots to keep viewers' respect. Instead of saying it was a bad shot, Williams countered, broadcasters can say, "I don't know if that's the shot they were looking for in that situation."

Johnson said that only works up to a certain point. "I will say that was a difficult shot," he said. "But if the player comes down and takes three more, me saying that was a difficult shot is not going to fly."

Williams, a Giant from 1987 to 1996, was voted by San Francisco fans in 1999 as the third baseman on the All-Giants San Francisco team. He ranks fifth in Giants home runs with 247, behind Willie Mays, Barry Bonds, Mel Ott, and Willie McCovey.

The third pick of the 1986 draft, Williams made a quick rise through the minor leagues, joining the Giants in 1987. In the 1989 National League Championship Series against the Cubs, Williams hit .300 with two home runs and nine RBIs.

Williams had a breakout season the following year, batting .277, slugging 33 home runs and driving in 122 RBIs as he became an All-Star for the first of five times in his career. He had a shot at breaking Roger Maris' single-season home run record in 1994, hitting 43 home runs in 112 games, but a players' strike canceled the rest of the season. His defense was just as good as his offense, as he won three Gold Gloves with the Giants in the early 1990s.

After a last-place finish in 1996, the Giants traded the popular third baseman to the Cleveland Indians for infielders Jeff Kent and Jose Vizcaino, and pitchers Julian Tavarez and Joe Roa. Giants fans' outcry over losing Williams forced new general manager Brian Sabean to famously declare, "I am not an idiot." Ultimately, the trade helped both clubs as the Giants won their division in 1997. Williams led the Indians to the American League pennant and a dramatic World Series that the Florida Marlins won in seven games.

Because Williams wanted to be closer to his children, Cleveland traded the Paradise Valley, Arizona, resident to the expansion Diamondbacks in 1998, where he played the last six seasons of his career. In the team's second season, Williams led the D-Backs to the NL West title with a .303 average, 35 homers, and 142 RBIs.

In the 2001 World Series against the Yankees, Williams batted .269 with one homer and seven RBIs. When Luis Gonzalez blooped the Series-winning hit, scoring Jay Bell from third, Williams was the first to rush to home plate to hug Bell in celebration. "It's the culmination of anything you would ever hope for," he said. "We got swept by the A's and lost to the Marlins in extra innings. To finally win, there's no feeling like it."

Williams suffered from leg and foot injuries the last few years of his career, including a broken foot in 2000 and a broken ankle that cost him half the year in 2002. He finished his 17-year career with a .268 average, 378 home runs, and 1,218 RBIs.

Radio host Williams (top left) talks with guest
Mike Prusinski (center) and co-host Roy Garibaldi.
Photo by Wylie Wong

Former Diamondbacks teammate Mark Grace said Williams was a team leader who put up Hall of Fame numbers, never showed up an opponent and carried himself with class and dignity. Williams spoke in soft tones, but his words of wisdom made everyone on the team listen and follow his lead.

"We looked to see how Matty handled situations. He never got too high and never got too low," Grace said. "When we won the first two World Series games, he was the guy who said, 'We still have to win two more. We haven't won anything yet,' He kept you grounded. But he also knew when it was time to get elated, too."

Williams remembers the thunderous applause fans at Candlestick Park gave him in 1999 as he walked out of the visiting Diamondbacks' dugout to join the other players that fans elected as all-time San Francisco Giants. Fearful of upsetting his teammates, he debated whether to wear a Giants uniform for the occasion. The D-Backs didn't object, so when the time came, he trotted onto the field in a Giants jersey.

"I didn't think at the time that I really warranted that. There are some great third basemen that played there, like Jim Ray Hart," Williams said of his selection. "So, it's an honor. I cherish that to this day."

Now more than a year into his retirement, Williams keeps busy and doesn't look back. "I miss the competition," he said. "But I don't miss the grind."

He married Phoenix TV news anchor Erika Monroe in 2003. They have a daughter to go along with Williams' three children. Besides the sports talk show, Williams in 2004 launched a stone importing company and a home design and construction business. With a business partner in Los Angeles, he imported stone from China and sold prefabricated countertops out of marble and specialty stones to contractors and hotels.

He also started a home design and construction business in Sun City, a fast-growing suburb west of Phoenix. "We cater to every need. We do everything from kitchen, bathrooms, backyards, everything," he said.

Williams was the president of both companies, while his partners served as the general managers who ran day-to-day operations. "I have so many things going on that I couldn't have time to be there every day," he said. "They essentially run it. I try to put deals together and help the business in that respect."

He also launched Matt Williams Baseball, a non-profit youth baseball league with about 1,600 kids participating in two Phoenix suburbs, Mesa and Chandler. It will soon expand to eight other cities in the Phoenix area.

On a typical day, Williams would wake up at 5:30 A.M. and take the kids to school. He worked on his two businesses in the morning and early afternoon. On the days he would do the radio show, he arrived at 3 P.M., an hour before the show, to prepare. Then it's home for dinner. He would drive his children to sports practice or singing and dancing lessons, then it's off to bed by 10 p.m.

Williams announced a few games on Giants television in 2004. During one game, Giants announcer Duane Kuiper remarked that former Diamondback Steve Finley—recently traded to the Dodgers for the stretch drive—looked strange in Dodger blue. Williams' response was sure to bring a chuckle to fans of the orange and black. "I'm an ex-Giant," Williams said. "So anybody looks bad in a Dodger uniform."

Williams wouldn't mind filling in as a game broadcaster on occasion, but he isn't ready to step into a full-time broadcasting role. It's the same reason he has no plans to return to the majors to coach anytime soon. He wants to spend time with his children.

"I missed a lot of time with my family [when I was] playing," Williams said. "I have three teenagers and a baby. I can't be leaving again."

For now, he will focus his broadcasting efforts on the sports talk show and help Garibaldi with his goal of syndicating the show throughout the United States. Williams co-hosts the show on Monday and Tuesdays, while a large roster of former professional athletes co-host on other days, including former Phoenix Suns basketball star Charles Barkley and former Phoenix Cardinals football player Seth Joyner.

Despite the show's title, its discussions are not always positive. In fact, the athletes who co-host the show sometimes rip other players. "We're not always perfect when we say we're positive. There are some things that we really agree

Though Williams has two businesses and four children,
he found time to broadcast a few Giants games in 2004.
Photo by Matt Johanson

with that athletes shouldn't be doing," Garibaldi said. "Some things in the negative we really agree with. But an athlete will say it. For a non-athlete to criticize an athlete that's never experienced it, I think is wrong."

Case in point, when the topic of the Athens Games came up, Williams said he was bothered that a few gold medalists were stripped of their medals after failing drug tests, robbing the silver medalist of the glory during the awards ceremony. Olympics officials should finalize drug tests results before the competition begins.

"These athletes compete for the opportunity to stand in the highest part of the podium and to have their flag higher than everyone else's, and hear the national anthem play," he said. "If the gold medalist tests positive, that silver medalist never gets to have that experience. It's more than the medal. It's the experience, being able to stand highest on that podium is what it's all about."

During a commercial break, Williams said he doesn't pretend to know everything and likes debating the issues. "I'm not an expert," he said. "You can be educated. You learn something new every day."

He also enjoys interacting with callers who once rooted for him on the field. "I think the biggest surprise has been callers calling in to say, 'I didn't think you were this way,'" Williams said. "When I played, I wasn't the best player, so I really had to concentrate on my job. I didn't talk a lot back then. So they have a different opinion of me now that I speak."

Williams has returned to baseball and is the current third base coach for the Arizona Diamondbacks. He's served on the D-Backs' coaching staff since 2010.

BRIAN JOHNSON

STARTS 'EM UP

In his off-seasons, Brian Johnson taught diversity training to corporate employees. He tutored youngsters at a Chicago elementary school, and even worked as a bank auditor one winter. The catcher knew he wouldn't play baseball forever, so when other players vacationed, he kept busy exploring future careers.

"I knew I never wanted to fall into the trap of being 'the athlete.' I've always looked for another career," said Johnson, an Oakland native and Stanford University graduate. "Unless I go out and do things, how else will I know what I will do when baseball is over?"

In 2004, Johnson, a hero during the Giants' 1997 playoff chase, was busy launching two businesses, while he worked in sales for Nike. He was a partner for a start-up athletics shoe and apparel store aimed at low-income neighborhoods, which will give inner-city youth much-needed jobs. He also developed a life skills training and crisis management service for potential clients that range from Major League Baseball and collegiate athletic programs to war veterans.

For baseball, Johnson envisioned embedding a former player into every team to serve as a mentor for players. The program would provide counseling for players with drug, alcohol, or other personal problems and help transition Latin American players into American life. For players who don't become stars and retire permanently wealthy, the program would help them secure off-season internships, so they can prepare for a career after baseball.

"In the big leagues and the minor leagues, it intrigued me that there were always some consistencies to the struggles and challenges that players had," he said. "This is to teach them to protect themselves: what agents and financial advisors should do for them. How to deal with people who assume you have money. You are away from home for eight months out of the year, so we'll have seminars on marital and family relationships. In a nutshell, we're developing the

*Noted Dodger-killer Brian Johnson helped
the Giants win a division title in 1997.*
© S.F. Giants

person that is the player."

Except for his foray into bank auditing, Johnson's career interests outside of sports have several common themes: education, multiculturalism, and helping those in need. At Stanford, Johnson even developed a tutoring program for low-income children in East Palo Alto.

Former Giants manager Dusty Baker, who befriended Johnson when he was a baseball and football star at Stanford, said Johnson's upbringing in ethnically diverse Oakland made him sensitive to these issues. In fact, his wife, a doctor, is African American. So while a white guy teaching diversity training may sound strange, Johnson can pull it off because of his background, his friends say.

"That's how he is as a person. He's kind of an international, universal type person," Baker said. "He's not judgmental, he's highly intelligent and able to communicate."

Education is a big part of Johnson's life, if his off-season work is any indication. In the defining moment of his baseball career, he taught the Dodgers the meaning of pain.

The Giants and Dodgers were deadlocked 5-5 in the bottom of the 12th inning. First place was on the line. The Dodgers were one game up in the division with two weeks of the 1997 season left to play. If the Giants won, they would tie for first place. If they lost, they would fall two behind with nine games to go. The Giants needed to win.

As Johnson walked up to the plate, he was exhausted. So were the 52,140 fans at Candlestick. They were emotionally drained from the ups-and-downs of the four-hour game, still trying to recover from the gut-wrenching bases-loaded, no-out jam that Giants closer Rod Beck miraculously escaped in the tenth inning.

"Everyone was gasping for breath," recalled Johnson, who came to the Giants in a midseason trade that year. "I remember thinking I just needed to get on base. Get a hit, a double—something—and win this thing."

Dodger reliever Mark Guthrie fired a fastball down the heart of the plate and Johnson crushed it. He knew it was gone immediately. The ball sailed into the left-field bleachers, and an ecstatic Johnson rounded the bases with his fists pumping in the air. When he reached home plate, he jumped into the arms of his teammates as the fans went delirious in unison.

"It was as if I were in a bubble. A force field," he said. "I could see everything. I could feel the vibrations. I knew it was loud, but what I was experiencing was a peaceful moment."

It wasn't just a SportsCenter highlight for one evening. It's a replay that's part of Giants lore forever. It was also a storybook ending to a game for a local kid who rooted for every Bay Area sports team while growing up, who graduated from Oakland's Skyline High School and was Stanford's starting quarterback in the late 1980s.

"That was a moment you'd have a hard time scripting," said former Giants announcer Ted Robinson. "It was wonderfully dramatic for a young guy who had grown up in the Bay Area, went to high school and college in the Bay Area, to finally come back home to play and deliver a hit to beat the archrival Dodgers in a pennant race game."

Johnson gets embarrassed by the attention he receives from the home run, but he enjoys reminiscing about it. "I'm so appreciative that people remember and I am associated with something positive," he said.

Six days after the blast against the Dodgers, Johnson slammed another game-winning homer in the ninth inning against Colorado. The Giants clinched the division a few days later.

In half a year with the Giants, Johnson batted .279 with 11 home runs and 27 RBIs. But he contributed more than just his bat in the 1997 season. Johnson quickly bonded with the pitching staff when he arrived in a midseason trade that was engineered by his friend Dusty Baker.

Johnson, who played for San Diego from 1994 to 1996, had started the season in Detroit, but had trouble adjusting to the American League. After 45 games, he batted only .237 with two homers and 18 RBIs and was sent down to Triple-A. Upset by the demotion, Johnson called up Baker, his mentor, and asked if he knew if any teams needed a catcher.

It turned out the Giants were seeking an alternative to catcher Rick Wilkins, who was batting .195 at the time. Baker talked to general manager Brian Sabean. Soon after, the Giants traded catcher Marcus Jensen to Detroit for Johnson.

Giants starter Kirk Rueter recalls Johnson spent a lot time and effort to get to know the pitchers, learn their tendencies and preferences, and gain their confidence.

"He did a great job catching. He was great to look to as far as the way he received the ball. He was always upbeat, always encouraging you," Rueter said. "He'd been around. It wasn't like he was a rookie catcher. He gained the pitchers' trust right away."

Johnson even got Rueter—who typically lives and dies on the outside corner—to throw inside to batters. Baker said Johnson, a former college quarterback, has natural leadership skills, which he used to manage the pitching staff.

Johnson's catching style was to take control, stay positive, and let the pitchers know that if they gave up hits or runs, Johnson took it personally. That built trust.

"Pitchers have so much to think about, where the leg and foot goes. If balls go high, what adjustments they have to make. The last thing they want to think about is what pitches to throw," he said. "But they're not going to hand over the reins of their career to somebody they don't trust. It's a huge challenge. You let them know you are thinking with them with every pitch. 'If you get hit, I get hit.' As that's gotten across, you are able to work with the pitcher."

Johnson relished the experience of calling a game. Like any catcher, he studied the scouting reports. But knowing the National League also helped. He knew the hitters, having spent his three previous years in San Diego. Before calling pitches, he took into account his pitchers' strengths and weaknesses, the hitters' previous at-bats, and how they were pitched to in the past.

"Kirk Rueter is different from Robb Nen and Mark Gardner. I'm able to adjust and call things that fit them," he said. "Not to toot my own horn, but not everyone takes as much time on the art of calling a game. Every game was like a story. The innings were the different scenes, and the pitches were the dialogue. Every pitch I called, there was a reason for it."

When pitchers were in a jam, Johnson's favorite technique was to paint a positive scenario on how to get out of it. "Pitchers want guidance in these situations," he said. "You get a positive plan of attack in their head and visualize that whole positive thing, and more times than not, good things will happen."

That happened in the '97 game against the Dodgers. When Beck gave up three straight singles to start the tenth inning, Johnson went to the mound and Beck asked him what they should do. Johnson told him they'd strike out Todd Zeile first. The next batter was Eddie Murray. "He's a first-pitch, dead red hitter," Johnson told Beck, using slang that means he's a fastball hitter. "Your split is working great. Let's throw the split-finger, he will roll it over to JK [Jeff Kent] for a double play, and we'll be out of it."

As it turned out, Zeile struck out and Murray hit a double-play grounder to Kent to end the inning, setting up Johnson's heroics in the 12th. "Rod believed this scenario was plausible. It was simple. It was positive, and it could be done. He said, 'Sounds good.' And it happened to turn out that way," Johnson said.

The next year, Johnson batted .237 with 13 home runs and 34 RBIs in a platoon with Brent Mayne. Even though Johnson didn't play as much as he wanted to, he remained a team player and didn't complain, Baker said. It didn't help that Johnson broke his hand twice, missing about a month each time.

"He didn't have as great a year in 1998, but he was still the same fun-loving guy," Rueter said. "It's always nice to play with people like that."

Johnson spent the last three years of his career jumping from team to team. He played for Cincinnati in 1999, Kansas City in 2000, and ironically enough, the Dodgers for three games in 2001. After eight big-league seasons, he retired with a career batting average of .248, 49 home runs and 196 RBIs.

Despite all his planning for a career after baseball, Johnson said he still went through the emotional struggle that most former professional athletes experience.

"It's a major trauma because a part of you has died," he said. "I've been focusing on perfecting one craft since I was six years old. Now 'I'm 33 and retired' when in reality, I'm starting all over again. It's that internal self-esteem struggle that begs the question, 'Can I do anything but play baseball? What will I do?' I wanted to do something I was passionate about, like I had been with my former

Johnson settled in Detroit with (from left)
his wife, Sarah, and their children, Alexandra and Zachary.
Brian Johnson family photo

career for 27 years."

He and his wife Sarah have settled in Detroit, where they raise their children. Johnson has continued to dabble in different careers. He's done some motivational speaking in schools. He worked for a non-profit company that helps schools raise funds. In 2004, he was busy getting his two companies off the ground.

He and his partners launched "Urban Legends Stadium," a start-up shoe and apparel company, with two components: direct sales of athletic gear and retail stores located in low-income communities. Johnson and his partners generated revenue by selling Nike products to school athletic teams and police and fire departments throughout the country.

The idea is to invest in low-income communities, help redevelop the neighborhoods and create new jobs, Johnson said.

"People go out to the suburban malls and that takes the money out of the community," he said. "Our stores will be embedded in their community."

During the summer of 2004, Johnson pitched the idea for a crisis prevention service to Major League Baseball and players' union officials and got positive responses.

"They feel this is a need and understand the importance of having a program like this," Johnson said. "Other former players have tried to get something going along these lines, but they had never seen anything as broad in scope and deep in detail as our proposal, so hopefully that will catapult us in there."

Johnson also planned to tailor the program to fit the needs of collegiate athletic programs and war veterans.

Johnson has warm memories of his time with the Giants, even though it lasted only two years. When he left San Francisco, he wrote a letter to Giants fans, thanking them for their support. He published the letter by purchasing ad space in every major Bay Area newspaper. Johnson said he did it because his Bay Area sports heroes never said goodbye when he was growing up.

"I always remembered when Kenny Stabler got traded to the Oilers, Dave Casper left and when Reggie Jackson went to New York," he said. "As a fan, I read about them. I watched them every day. I loved those guys, and when they left, they didn't say goodbye."

So he wanted to tell the Bay Area farewell and thank you.

"I always like to do things the way it should be done," he said. "When I was leaving, I felt it was premature. I wasn't happy about it. It was a unique way to give a piece of myself back."

After nine years in corporate America, Johnson was ready to get back into baseball. So in 2010, he re-joined the Giants as a scout, where he covers much of the Midwest region.

He's part of a group of 10 scouts that cover all 30 Major League teams and 150 Minor League teams. "I help on finding talent for us to trade for before the July 31st trade deadline or sign as a free agent in the off-season," he says. "I also help in our advance scouting to help Bruce Bochy and the rest of the team prepare, and hopefully defeat, the opponent."

Johnson has a long history with Brian Sabean, so when he was ready to return to baseball, the Giants general manager was the first person he called.

"I first met Sabes when he was the scouting director with the Yankees and I was a 16th-round draft choice for them in 1989. I was reunited with him in a mid-season trade to the Giants in 1997, where we all worked together and won a division championship," he says.

The 2013 marks his fourth season as a Giants scout, and he's enjoying the experience.

"The Giants are great about including the former Giants and allowing them to always feel a part of the Black and Orange family," Johnson says. "The Giants and Brian Sabean have always been good to me, and I am grateful."

JEFF KENT

FROM SECOND BASE TO "SURVIVOR"

Jeff Kent, the baseball star, is now Jeff Kent, the reality TV star. The former All-Star Giants second baseman, who retired from the sport four years ago, returned to the public eye during the 2012 fall TV season as a contestant on CBS' show "Survivor." Now, more than ever, people come up to him on the streets and say hello.

"I get recognized more from Survivor than as a baseball player. I hope it didn't re-define my career," Kent said in a recent phone interview.

For 39 days, he joined former "Facts of Life" TV star Lisa Whelchel and 16 other castaways on an island in the Philippines, hoping to outwit, outplay and outlast every one of them for the title of "Sole Survivor" and $1 million.

He almost didn't survive the first day. Within minutes of the game starting, he fell off a boat and onto a raft, tearing the MCL in his left knee. He gutted it out, however, and was highly competitive in challenges, seemingly running and swimming at full speed. A fierce competitor, Kent admits he was never the most social guy in a baseball clubhouse, but he was very social on Survivor, creating a tight alliance with several castaways, including 50-year-old writer Jonathan Penner.

During the show, he managed to keep his baseball identity a secret, choosing to tell people that he owned three motorcycle dealerships in central Texas, which was also true. "I was always telling half the truth out there. It was never all the truth," he says. "I was grateful they did not know who I was. I did not want to try to talk through the baggage of being a celebrity or a guy who made a lot of money in my career."

In the end, his alliances were not strong enough as he became the eighth person to get voted off the island. After getting ousted, he ranted to the TV cameras, saying: "You know what pissed me off? I think I've made about $60 million playing baseball, and I want this frickin' million dollars in this game and it's not even a million bucks! It's six hundred grand by the time Obama takes it. I'm a Game 7 World Series loser. You know, I've played in the biggest games in the world and the worst games in the world, but this just sucks.'"

His goodbye speech was as funny as it was a timely political statement, having aired days after President Obama's re-election. His rant lit up the sports blogs the day after and was later described by Survivor host Jeff Probst as probably the best exit speech ever in the show's 25 seasons.

For most Survivor fans, Kent was just another contestant. But for Giants fans, he was a major piece of the Giants' renaissance in the late 1990s and early 2000s, with the team making the playoffs three times and nearly winning the World Series in 2002.

Kent arrived before the 1997 season in an off-season trade that sent Matt Williams to Cleveland, and upon his arrival, the power-hitting second baseman promptly hit .250 with 29 home runs and 121 RBIs, helping lead the Giants to the National League West division crown. In 2000, he won the National League Most Valuable Player award after a .334, 33 home run, 125 RBI season. Overall, he drove more than 100 RBIs in each of his six seasons in San Francisco.

After leaving the Giants after the 2002 season, he had six more productive years with the Astros and the Dodgers before retiring. Despite playing for six teams in his 17-year career, he says his time in San Francisco was the highlight of his career. He's even back in the Giants fold, serving as a part-time Spring Training instructor the past three years. Today, he lives in the Austin, Texas area with his wife and four children.

In a question-and-answer interview, Kent discusses why he went on *Survivor*, he talks about his time in San Francisco, and shares whether he plans to do more reality TV in the future.

Q: I understand you are a long-time fan of Survivor. *But a lot of people are fans and have no interest in being on the show. What made you want to do it and take on the challenge?*

Kent: I am a competitor. I always have been. Baseball was my fix to be competitive, so I was challenged to be on the show. I like the show. It's the biggest show that's captured my attention throughout my years of watching TV. I'm an outdoors guy. I'm a scout leader now with the youth in my church. I've always been a guy who likes to camp out and explore and survive off the land. What a great controlled atmosphere for me to participate in and compete at a level of trying to survive.

Q: How grueling was the experience? Every episode, we only see one hour of three days. Was it hard being away from family, going off the grid with no technology, barely having any food, and sitting for hours on end in the rain?

Kent: Being away from the family was the biggest challenge. We were gone for a long period of time without contact. I don't think it was grueling. For me, I wish it was harder physically because if it was harder, other people would fall off the table, and I'd have a better go of it. I would not have been kicked off the island so soon.

The beaches we were on were pleasant and the ocean water was warm, albeit it rained for 15 days straight. That was tough. But because we had rain, we had fresh water. The ocean was swimmable. We had enough food. Yeah, we were hungry, but we were not starving to the point we were desperate.

Q: But did it feel like camping, though?
Kent: At the beginning it did because you are not panicked about surviving the game socially. You are setting yourself up and making your camp, gathering the food, and making sure you have enough firewood. You're trying to make fire and get a rhythm of when to cook food, how much to hold back on the rations, so you map how much you can eat every day. I'd say the first five, six, or seven days felt like camping without the luxuries of camping.

Day to day was somewhat simple. You don't have the challenges of the grind at home, where you have to answer e-mails and go grocery shopping. You basically have one set of clothes. You go to bed when it gets too dark and you wake up when it's light enough to see. You are kind of foraging around for food and planning your days around the challenges. You sit around much of the day just jibber-jabbering with your tribemates. You try to get a feel for them, get an understanding if they are truthful or not. You are strategizing how to align with people and better position yourself, so you are not the next to get voted out.

Q: How did you prepare for Survivor?
Kent: So many people get caught up looking good for the TV cameras and wanting to look buff and lean and mean and have a good tan. For me, I stayed the same, doing the things I normally do, like a little bit of running. I didn't worry so much about my weight because I knew I would need it.

Q: What are some of your favorite memories of the experience?
Kent: Some of the big memories I have are doing the challenges with my teammates. Winning some of the challenges with Penner. We were able to whip right through the puzzles. Those challenges I really liked and they were fun.

Q: Is there anything from your baseball career that helped you with Survivor?
Kent: Being in different locker rooms on all the different teams I played on and being able to communicate with guys with different personalities. And being

able to handle stressful situations and being able to control my emotions. Those things helped me on the island because Survivor is such a big social game and I think that helped me.

Q: You have said the toughest part of playing Survivor *was the social game. But on TV, it seemed like you were incredibly social. It looked like you had a strong alliance. You were always strategizing and talking to people, even with people in the other alliance. Can you talk about the social game?*

Kent: Well, thank you for that comment. Throughout my baseball career, I had been a guy who's been pretty quiet and when I open my mouth, most of the time I can get in trouble because I tell too much of the truth. Or, there are times when I tell people, 'I don't want to talk to you, so go away,' and that could frustrate people. There are also times when I wanted to focus on playing baseball and that did not require me to be social, so I wasn't very social, and I think people understood me to be aloof, if you will, to be unsociable, to be selfish. And that was so far from the truth.

And yet on the game itself and playing on *Survivor*, I was able to not have to have that competitive edge. I did not need the anger, if you will, to drive me to success because I knew it was a social game. I knew I had to be social to get to the end, and I knew I needed my tribemates to do two things. One is to help me get to the end and, two is if I vote them off, I still need them to like me enough to vote me to be the winner at the end. I really believe that the show has done a fantastic job of showing the reality of all the players. What you see of me on the show is who I am in real life. I just don't need the competitive edge of playing baseball anymore, so that's basically who I am.

Q: How's your knee? In an online video on CBS' Survivor *website after you were voted off, you mentioned that you did tear your MCL.*

Kent: I tore it. It's still sore, but I will get over it. It will just take a lot of time because it was a pretty big tear.

Q: In the early episodes, you talked about how you thought you tore your MCL. But then, you competed so well in challenges, I think viewers thought, 'Oh, OK, he's OK.'

Kent: (Laughter.) I had to. If my teammates thought I was hurt, they would have smelled blood and they would have kicked me off. When I hurt my knee and I got on the island, everybody was in my face, 'how's your knee? Are you OK? Can you help us in challenges?' I was getting grilled. I had to turn it around really fast and put up with the pain and say, 'You know what? I'm OK.'

All the challenges that I did, I did around my knee. Swimming was OK. It hurt a little bit. Anything that I did straight away, I had no problem because it was my inside ligament on my left knee. One of the challenges was where you catch balls in the air with a net. That one hurt bad because I had to do side-to-side, lateral stuff. We were trying to zig zag and run around and jump to catch the thing. I had a hard time doing that one. I knew we were not going to win, so I didn't put in 100 percent. I knew I was safe and knew I would not get voted off, so I protected my knee there, so I could be better for the next day. That's how I got around my knee injury.

Q. After being voted off, they showed a clip of you talking about how upset you were at not winning. Are you still upset at not winning – or has time smoothed things over?
Kent: (Laughter.) It stays with you. You spend a lot of time and sacrifice and suffering out there to win a game and when it's taken from you for reasons that are not logical, you really scratch your head and you get ticked off. I am a competitor. I love to win, but I'm not bitter about it.

Even though it happened in the spring, you watch it again [when it airs on TV] and you relive it. And it still makes you mad. That's what great about this game. It stays with you. You still go through, 'if I could have done this, maybe I could have still been there.' That's how contagious this game is. It sticks with you. You still get upset even though it's months later.

Q: You played with three returning players, so it's possible they will ask you to do the show again. Knowing what you know now, would you do the show again? Kent: I had a great time there. I didn't win. I didn't accomplish my goal. If I were asked again to do it, I would probably say yes because I have unfinished business.

Q: Would you do other shows like Amazing Race?
Kent: *Amazing Race* is a show I've watched, too. That would be kind of fun, too. My wife and I crack about that show. That she would never do it with me because I would be wearing her out every day. (Laughter.) We would probably end up getting divorced after that show. (Laughter.)

Q: What response did you get from your former baseball teammates? Did they tease or joke around with you as the season progressed?
Kent: They teased me. It's been fun. They say, 'Don't you have anything better to do?' I've been getting a lot of jabs along the lines of, 'Are you kidding me? That's all you got?'

Q: A lot of Giants fans remember the 2002 World Series and how bitter that loss was. At the 10th year anniversary of the World Series team at AT&T Park, you gave *a great speech. You told the crowd and I quote, "2002 was the greatest time of my life. Baseball players play this game either for two reasons: to make history, or another, to be a champion. There was no doubt when we left here after Game 5 of the 2002 World Series... we all knew in our hearts that we would bring you back that trophy. Just a few years later, you got that trophy now. This city is world champions, and I'm proud of that."*

Kent: I meant every word of it. The fans deserved it. In 1997, I watched the fans come out to Candlestick Park and suffer through the weather – suffer through the old stadium – to watch the Giants play. And when we moved to the new ballpark, it would sell out every day. The city gave us so much support. They deserved it. I was happy when they finally got the trophy.

Q: How do you view your time in San Francisco?

Kent: I loved playing there. My career blossomed there. Of all the teams I played for, San Francisco was the only place where I bought a home. My kids went to school there. San Francisco was our home. We had block parties with neighbors. It was cool to have that atmosphere.

Q: What is your role with the Giants now?

Kent: I go to Spring Training. I help if anyone needs special instruction. I don't have a title. I'm on their speed dial anytime they need me.

Q: One more thing I want to tell you before I let you go. My brother has a signed baseball bat from you that he won at a silent auction during a fund-raiser in 2000 or 2001. He wants to tell you that it's in his living room, and if intruders ever come in, he's going to use it to start busting heads.

Kent: (Laughter.) You tell him to hit them in the sweet spot. It's all ready for him.

GOLDEN REFLECTIONS

MUSINGS ON THE 2010 AND 2012 WORLD SERIES TITLES

S an Francisco's World Series victories in 2010 and 2012 ended more than five decades of waiting and exhilarated millions of fans. They also carried special meaning to Giants' alumni who laid the foundations for the championships. Here are some of their thoughts about the orange and black titles.

Members of the 2010 Giants raise San Francisco's first World Series trophy.
Matt Johanson

"It was just great. I got to be a small part of that. I've been fortunate to be with the Giants team for an awful long time, and being with the world championship team is certainly one of my greatest highlights with the Giants."

—Jim Davenport, Giants infielder, 1958-1970

"They've got heart. They didn't have a superstar on the club. They played together. This was about 25 guys pulling for each other. That's what makes a great ballclub. I'm so proud of them."

—Willie Mays, Giants outfielder 1951-1972

"The success the Giants have experienced the last couple of years, I think, is gratifying for any of us associated with the team or worked at Candlestick, whether we were baseball players, front office people, ticket takers, parking attendants or concession stand workers. It brought a lot of pride to all of us, especially for someone like myself where the orange and black gave me the first opportunity to compete in pro baseball."

—Dave Heaverlo, Giants pitcher 1975-1977

"Believe it or not, after all these years, hardly a day goes by that someone doesn't bring that up that line drive to Bobby Richardson. I had a chance and I didn't get it done in '62. I like to think that these guys did it for me. They came through for me."

—Willie McCovey, Giants infielder/outfielder 1959-1973, 1977-1980

"Watching the games made me feel good. They just went out and played, things went right and they won. It was a lot of fun for myself as a former player and also as a Giants fan."

—Jim Barr, Giants pitcher 1971-1978, 1983

"I enjoyed San Francisco winning it all. The organization and especially the fans waited a long time for this moment. Well deserved. Don't ask me why, but I thought of Bob Lurie, who bought the Giants, thus preventing them from moving to Toronto. I bet he's happy."

—Ed Halicki, Giants pitcher 1974-1980

"The Giants showed their strength in both the 2010 and 2012 world Championship seasons: pitching, pitching, pitching! The starting rotation and bullpen were the corner stone for each championship. A relentless will to win was inscribed in each player in the drive to be the best."

—Bill Laskey, Giants pitcher 1982-1985

Duane Kuiper and Mike Krukow fired up fans at the championship celebrations.
Matt Johanson

"I came to this organization in 1982 and I only knew a couple of things about it. One, it had a really bad ballpark. It used to have a center fielder by the name of Willie Mays. I also knew that it had never won a world championship. So my torture started in 1982 and I'm happy to say that, thanks to these gentlemen, the torture is over!"

—Duane Kuiper, Giants infielder 1982-1985

"The wonderful thing in all of this is how humble these guys were. They pooled together and that reflected the character of the Giants organization through their play. I thought that was amazing with the adversity they went through. They endured. They kept fighting game after game. Everyone deflected personal praise. They were focused in this whole idea of the team. And suddenly you heard conversation and dialogue about how important the fans were to this season. When you start giving credit in those areas and deflect from yourself, that says so much about the 2010 and 2012 teams."

—Dave Dravecky, Giants pitcher 1987-1989

"I didn't think they had the best team [in 2010], but they have an outstanding manager. They did a great job like the team [in 2012]. They never let up and

it was a real team effort and they outplayed them."
                          —Roger Craig, Giants manager 1985-1992

"When I look back on the ultimate victories on the big stage in 2010 and 2012, I think of the cutting-edge approach that the baseball department has developed. 'Moneyball 2' could be written today showing the newest evolution of the game and the logo on the marquee would be that of the San Francisco Giants.

"In today's game, teams must be able to evaluate the play and the player on field more in depth and intensely than ever before. Numbers are important, but one could do every analysis and number crunching without ever viewing one baseball game on the field in person. In today's game, teams must be able to draft, hone and grow their own talent. They must be able to identify and nurture leaders on the field and they must be able to project skills, character and personalities. They also must be able to properly assess potential free agents with shrewdness based on necessity versus falling in love with the newest media darling. This is what the Giants do better than any other modern day major league baseball organization.

"The world championships two out of the last three seasons are no fluke. They are the direct result of combining baseball intelligence and human assessment, with a sprinkle of numbers to support your case. This is what the victories mean to me as a fan, a former player, a scout and a baseball lifer."
                          —Brian Johnson, Giants catcher 1997-1998

"I'm jealous. I'm jealous because they played so well. They made it look so easy. I'm so proud of what they've done. I'm happy for them. I'm proud that I can continue to be a part of the organization in the small capacity that I am now. I am proud to say I played for the Giants organization, and now they are two-time World Champions in a short period of time. I'm also proud for some of the players because they've got some good ones. I'm happy for them, albeit selfishly, I'm jealous because I wasn't there."
                          —Jeff Kent, Giants infielder 1997-2002

"I'm blown away. This has got to be the greatest thing for the city. I'm so happy for the city, happy for the fans, and happy for the Giants."
                          —Barry Bonds, Giants outfielder 1993-2007

BIBLIOGRAPHY

Bitker, Steve. *The Original San Francisco Giants: The Giants of '58.* Champaign, Illinois: Sports Publishing Inc., 1998.

Cepeda, Orlando and Herb Fagen. *Baby Bull: From Hardball to Hard Time and Back.* Dallas: Taylor Publishing Company, 1998.

Dark, Alvin and John Underwood. *When in Doubt, Fire the Manager: My Life and Times in Baseball.* New York: Dutton, 1980.

Dickey, Glenn. *San Francisco Giants: 40 Years.* San Francisco: Woodford Press, 1997.

Forman, Sean L. *Baseball-Reference.com—Major League Statistics and Information.* http://www.baseball-reference.com, 2004.

Mays, Willie and Lou Sahadi. *Say Hey: The Autobiography of Willie Mays.* New York: Pocket Books, 1989.

Perry, Gaylord and Bob Sudyk. *Me and the Spitter: An Autobiographical Confession.* New York: Saturday Review Press, 1974.

Schott, Tom and Nick Peters. *The Giants Encyclopedia.* Champaign, Illinois: Sports Publishing LLC, 2003.

Stein, Fred and Nick Peters. *Giants Diary.* Berkeley: North Atlantic Books, 1987.

8/18

NF